Historic Tales
of
DECATUR COUNTY
INDIANA

Historic Tales
of
DECATUR COUNTY
INDIANA

JOHN PRATT

THE
History
PRESS

Published by The History Press
Charleston, SC
www.historypress.com

Front cover, top: public domain; *bottom*: Will Lemay (photo released into the public domain).
Back cover: author collection; *insert*: courtesy of Decatur County Historical Society.

First published 2022

Manufactured in the United States

ISBN 9781467149327

Library of Congress Control Number: 2021952409

Notice: The information in this book is true and complete to the best of our knowledge. It is offered without guarantee on the part of the author or The History Press. The author and The History Press disclaim all liability in connection with the use of this book.

To my parents, Rex and Lucille Pratt, for taking me to my first fort and Abraham Lincoln historic site. I will always treasure our memories. To my wife, Jill, and daughters, Clare and Caroline. The three of you are my daily support and inspiration. I am honored to call you my family.

Jill and John Pratt. *Courtesy of Heather Comer.*

CONTENTS

Contents

ACKNOWLEDGEMENTS

For a novice to write any kind of book requires the help of many hands. This venture would not have been attempted without the aid of my chief supporter, lead typist and editor, my wife of thirty-three years, Jill Pratt. We are fortunate in our small town to have a vigorous Decatur County Historical Society, and Carrie Shoemaker and Charity Mitchell aided my research on numerous occasions. Thanks to my student Jenna Ankney for helping me type the calendar of events. *Greensburg Daily News* columnist Pat Smith was always willing to answer local history questions when needed. Daniel Fayette is a talented photographer who was kind enough to take the current photos used. Tracy Winters provided invaluable guidance on images.

INTRODUCTION

*T*here are 3,006 counties in the United States of America, and I chose to write about just one, Decatur County, Indiana. Why? Because it is my home. I was born and raised here, moved away for sixteen years and came back. I am a high school history teacher who sees tremendous value in sharing our local heritage with the next generation. This book contains my favorite stories that may interest my students. This is by no means meant to be a comprehensive history of Decatur County. Parts of this book are very personal to me. I find great value in making history personal, as it helps the people, places and events become more relevant to one's own life experiences.

There are certainly plenty of people who know more than I do about Decatur County's local history, but the lens I use needs to be one that motivates a group of people who are not easily interested in history: high school students. Many students may not be able to name five U.S. presidents, but they all know Abraham Lincoln. Hopefully, they will be able to picture Abe arriving in Greensburg on a train on February 12, 1861, his birthday. He is on his way to Washington to be sworn in as president of the United States during the most tumultuous time in our history. This is just one short story about a great man who stopped in Decatur County for only a few minutes as a favor to a friend who lived here. Many of the stories in this book are about people in this community overcoming obstacles to achieve great things. History is full of such people, but one may not realize they need look no farther than their own neighborhood to find them.

Part I

STORIES OF GREENSBURG AND DECATUR COUNTY THAT EVERYONE SHOULD KNOW

1

CHAUTAUQUA

THEN AND NOW

I was always a fan of history. I idolized Abraham Lincoln and even tried to make myself look like him as a kid. I grew up in a sports-minded family, which led me to collect baseball cards and learn more about our nation's pastime. In college, I majored in history. During my senior year, I needed to write a major research paper, and I chose my hometown to write about. I knew we had a famous tree in our courthouse and that the city was founded by a man named Thomas Hendricks. Surely there was enough to find to write a paper? There absolutely was! I found a treasure-trove of information about heroes from every war, famous dignitaries who visited, the connection between Abraham Lincoln and his friend Will Cumback, stories of the Underground Railroad and so much more. Then I learned a word that changed my life forever: *Chautauqua.* The word is from the Iroquois, meaning "two tied together," as well as "bag tied in the middle." The Iroquois gave that name to Chautauqua Lake in western New York. The lake looks like it has a bag tied in the middle of it. It seemed the perfect location for Lewis Miller and John Vincent to build their vision of a summer Sunday school training facility in 1874. The two were heavily influenced by the Lyceum movement from earlier in the nineteenth century, which brought great lecturers from Mark Twain to Ralph Waldo Emerson across the country. In the 1870s, people were hungry for more of this type of entertainment, which included inspirational sermons, music and recreational sports. The new vision of Chautauqua quickly became popular. The iconic institution continues to thrive to this day as a beacon for the finest in arts and culture.

North Decatur High School Chautauqua with, from left to right, Gary Cook, Coach Bill Yoast from *Remember the Titans*, John Pratt, Vince Papale from *Invincible* and Rod Hite. *Author collection.*

Things get interesting in the early part of the twentieth century as the traveling Chautauqua emerged. Communities across the country wanted to experience what Teddy Roosevelt called "the most American thing about America." Greensburg, Indiana, provided a good example of how things operated. A local organization was created in 1911, and it contracted with two promoters from Bloomington, Illinois, James L. Loar and James Shaw. It was Loar and Shaw's job to provide the headline entertainers and speakers; the local community would add homegrown talent. The first Greensburg Chautauqua took place from July 1 to 9, 1911, in a part of town referred to as Brackens' Woods. The headline speakers that year were Spanish-American War hero Captain Richard F. Hobsen, as well as the inspirational T.P. Gore, a blind senator from Oklahoma. What ensued was a wonderful new annual tradition.

In its fourth year, the local event moved to the big top, as tents were set up on the site that would later become Billings Elementary School, now the Greensburg City Hall. The icon of the traveling Chautauquas was William

Chautauqua 2017.
Author collection.

Jennings Bryan, a three-time presidential candidate. He wowed the local audience in 1912 with his "The Prince of Peace" speech and returned by popular demand in 1922 with "Brute or Brother." The most memorable speaker in the twenty-year run had to be Helen Keller.

The popularity of Chautauqua in Decatur County was not limited to Greensburg. Events were held in Westport, Letts and Clarksburg, among others. The Burney Chautauqua once hosted John Philip Sousa. In 1931, the Greensburg Chautauqua was notified that the promoters were shutting down. Competition from radio and the movies was just too great for the traveling Chautauquas to survive. As the local group met for the last time, it was stated, "And the Chautauqua will doubtless never come back." But that was not entirely accurate.

I first learned about the Greensburg Chautauqua's history while doing research for a college history project on Greensburg. I was amazed to read about inspirational speakers like Helen Keller who spoke in little ol' Greensburg, Indiana. The Chautauqua stage was also filled with music concerts. I thought it was a terrible shame that it ended in 1930. Still, the idea of Chautauqua made a lasting impression on me as a twenty-one-year-old.

It has been said the average person changes their career seven times during their lifetime. At the age of forty-three, I walked into a classroom for the first time as a social studies teacher. It was a job that came naturally to me, and with great students and tremendously supportive staff, I knew I had made the right choice. Still, with such a major emphasis on high-stakes standardized tests, I felt that students were missing out on something. I finally decided that this was good, old-fashioned inspiration. Sure, there were great teachers, but what else could I do? My first idea was to create a questionnaire in the hopes of asking some culturally and historically significant people to respond. To my surprise, some did. After that, I added a line that asked if they would be willing to do a short phone interview with students. When I was able to host an interview for my students with Earl Hamner Jr., the creator of the television series *The Waltons* and the model for the character John Boy, I knew I was on to something. Since then, I have hosted nearly four hundred phone, Skype and Zoom interviews. Some of my favorites have been Condoleezza Rice, Lech Wałęsa, James Patterson, Ted Sorensen, Norman Bridwell, Robert Indiana, Brenda Lee, Bruce Hornsby, Denny Miller, Bill Guarnere (depicted in the miniseries *Band of Brothers*), Zbigniew Brzezinski, Grace Slick, Tony Shalhoub, Vanna White, Nick Offerman, Greta Friedman (the nurse kissed on the cover of *LIFE* magazine in 1945), Phyllis Reynolds Naylor, Monte Irvin and Donna Shalala. All of these interviews had surpassed my expectations, but I wanted to take it to the next level. What else could I do to provide inspiration for my students? I remember exactly where I was in my second semester at North Decatur High School when it hit me. I needed to organize another Chautauqua in Decatur County! I remembered learning about it in college and how amazed I was not only by the depth that arts and culture played in the community but also that famous individuals were speaking and performing right here in our neck of the woods. If past organizers could do it, so could I! So, in my second semester of teaching, the first Chautauqua event in a school was born.

We had no money, so we were very fortunate to have Allison and Cory Bickel, two amazing opera singers, as our headliners. The format hasn't changed in twenty-six events. During the day, there are great historically and culturally significant speakers; at night, a program is presented designed for the community. I'll never forget the second semiannual event, as we raised enough money for a plane ticket for a very special guest, Rosemarie von Trapp. She was one of the original von Trapp family children and singers. She entertained and delighted everyone as she sang songs from *The Sound of Music*.

I treasure the memories of those nine events at North Decatur. Each event grew in stature. Before too long, people even knew how to pronounce "Chautauqua." A number of themed events took place at North Decatur. The theme African American Achievements featured three Freedom Riders, two baseball players from the Negro Leagues, an original plaintiff from 1954's *Brown v. Board of Education* and a member of the Supremes. All of this culminated in the renovation of an abandoned AME cemetery. Persons buried there had been conductors on the Underground Railroad.

World War II: Heroes and Survivors was another special Chautauqua theme. Survivors from the USS *Indianapolis* and Pearl Harbor shared their harrowing tales. A POW who worked near the River Kwai, and Paul Argiewicz, a Holocaust survivor, shared their stories as well. There was also a Tuskegee Airman, a woman who flew in the U.S. Air Force (WASP), a fighter ace and a member of the Belski Partisans, Polish Jews who fought back against the Nazis. Other highlights from the nine North Decatur events included visits from Katie Stamm, Miss America from Seymour, Indiana; Coach Bill Yoast, who was depicted in the movie *Remember the Titans*; Vince Papale, depicted in the movie *Invincible*; a member of the Little Rock Nine; a September 11 survivor; and Pulitzer Prize–winning photographer Nick Ut.

It was a wonderful five years at North Decatur, but the move to my alma mater allowed me to expand Chautauqua and other programs that I had created. I will never forget my first event in the John W. Goddard Auditorium. On the same stage were six Holocaust survivors, among others. Here, too, there were memorable themes such as Music, which included Tony-nominated performer Liz Callaway and Woodstock performer Nancy Nevins. The Hollywood theme saw stars from TV and film, from *It's a Wonderful Life* and *Pirates of the Caribbean* to *The Gilmore Girls* and *The Walking Dead*, along with holiday favorites such as *A House without a Christmas Tree* and *A Christmas Story*.

The biggest crowd we ever had was when Emmy winner Ed Asner took to the stage. Following close behind him was the remarkable Mike Farrell, who played B.J. Honeycutt on *MASH*, and everyone's favorite singing cowboys, Riders in the Sky. Chautauqua has hosted guests from seven other countries, including Nobel Peace laureate Leymah Gbowee (Liberia); Benjamin Mee from Great Britain, who was depicted in the movie *We Bought a Zoo*; the last Nazi hunter, Dr. Efraim Zuroff from Israel; and many others.

With each Chautauqua that I host, students in my classes are assigned one major project based on their skills and interests. Many projects have been showstoppers. Kaitlynn Scheidler wanted to learn more about 9/11, so she set out on a quest to interview survivors who had been buried in the rubble. She astonishingly interviewed nineteen of the twenty-two she sought. The survivors were so impressed with her project that they invited Katelynn and her family to New York for the fifteenth-anniversary memorial event. Another project that stood out was a fundraising motorcycle ride created by Kheirsten Hess, whom I nicknamed "Peppy." I have had many students conduct fundraisers, and they have been mostly very successful. Peppy's event topped them all, as she single-handedly raised $10,000 for a domestic violence shelter. Her program still exists today and seeks creative ways to support veterans as well.

I describe Chautauqua as a celebration of diversity and the greatness that exists in all of us. I believe it has accomplished that. Even being forced to go virtual due to the COVID pandemic, we were able to host Dr. Jane Goodall, as well as a concert series. I hope the Chautauqua I have brought to Decatur County over the years honors Chautauquas of the past and continues to bring something of value to the community for many more years.

2

WILL CUMBACK

NOTED STATESMAN AND FRIEND OF ABRAHAM LINCOLN

*A*s a senior in college, my capstone class as a history major was called Historiography. It was in this class that each student chose a topic on which to do an in-depth paper. I loved history and my hometown, and I knew about our famous tree, so I decided to write about Greensburg, Indiana. I called it "A Tree Grows in Greensburg." I have always found value in learning one's heritage, whether it is a family tree or a hometown history. I believe it helps ground a person, helping them to learn to appreciate those who came before. To say that my research was eye-opening is an understatement. I couldn't believe that someone from Greensburg was a close friend of the greatest American president, Abraham Lincoln. That man was Will Cumback, and this is a bit of his story.

Will Cumback was born near Mount Caramel in Franklin County, Indiana, in March 1829. After receiving his bachelor's degree from Miami of Ohio and his law degree from the University of Cincinnati, he moved to Greensburg and joined the bar in 1853. Beginning his political career did not take long. The young attorney was a member of the Whig Party until it ceased to exist in the early 1850s. In 1854, he successfully won election to the U.S. House of Representatives with the transitional Opposition Party. Members of this party were opposed to the spread of slavery in the United States. Cumback quickly rose to national prominence. His 1856 rebuke of the U.S. Supreme Court's Dred Scott decision earned him high praise on the floor of the House, but his bid for reelection was unsuccessful.

Back home in Indiana, Will was on the ground floor of the new Republican Party, much like his political friend in Illinois, Abraham Lincoln. He campaigned long and hard for the rail-splitter from Springfield in the 1860 presidential campaign. In fact, it was none other than Will Cumback who cast Indiana's first Republican electoral vote, that going to Lincoln. Cumback would look at that moment as his greatest political contribution.

It is hard to imagine what this country would look like today had Abraham Lincoln not been elected president in 1860. It was shortly after his inauguration that the first shots were fired at Fort Sumter, signaling the beginning of the Civil War. President Lincoln called for volunteers to squelch the rebellion, hoping a ninety-day enlistment would be enough. Even with all of his ambitions and political clout, Will volunteered as a private with the Seventh Indiana Regiment, which played a successful role in the creation of a new Union state, West Virginia. At the end of the ninety days, Will left the regiment as a lieutenant colonel. It was then that Lincoln requested his service to act as one of four Union paymasters, a role Will dutifully performed for the duration of the war. At the conclusion of the Civil War, his books balanced to the penny. It was time to go back home to Indiana.

In 1866, Will was elected to the Indiana senate, and the following year he was made president of that body. In 1868, he was successful in his bid to be elected lieutenant governor. President Ulysses Grant came calling in 1871 with an offer of the ambassadorship to Portugal, but Will declined it in order to move back home to Greensburg, where he accepted an offer to work for the Internal Revenue Service. But Will remained active in politics. During the Republican Convention of 1876, when it became obvious that Indiana governor Oliver Morton would not receive the nomination for president; Will convinced the Indiana delegation to support Rutherford B. Hayes. This led to Hayes's nomination and subsequent presidency. Cumback also played important roles in local community affairs. These included a leadership role in the Methodist Church as well as serving as the first president of the Greensburg Public Library.

I think it is important to note that Will Cumback was much more than a successful politician. He contributed greatly to his community and nation. He was in high demand nationwide as a speaker. He is the only Decatur Countian to have spoken at the Chautauqua Institute in New York. Finally, he was a noted writer and poet. I believe Will Cumback is the greatest statesman this community has ever produced.

Above: Will Cumback House. *Author collection.*

Left: Abraham Lincoln letter to Will Cumback. *Author collection.*

The following is a poem written by Will Cumback.

A Sabbath Day

Like a mother's kiss to the weary child,
Like the calm sea waves, raging and wild,
Like rest, sweet rest, to tired feet,
Like joy's sweet dream while sorrows sleep,
Like dew upon the drooping flower,
Like hope in a despairing hour,
Like joyful news from those we love,
Like benedictions from above,
Comes the Sabbath morn to me.

3

ELIZABETH FINNERN

THE ONLY WOMAN BURIED IN
SOUTH PARK CEMETERY'S SOLDIERS CIRCLE

Like many others, I have always been fascinated by the Civil War. That interest in the history of the battles of the North versus the South has grown over the years, partly because of my passion for local history stories. A great place to start is South Park Cemetery. As you enter through the main gate off East Street, you will see straight ahead the beautiful Soldiers Circle. On Memorial Day each year, with all of the flags and flowers, it is just like a Norman Rockwell painting. As you pay your respects to all of the fallen soldiers, you will soon notice one marker off to the right that is not like the others; in fact, a married couple is buried there. The husband's name was John Finnern, and his wife's name was Elizabeth. Hers is an amazing story.

It is true that many things in life can be taken for granted; health, food, clothing, shelter. Our freedom is another such thing, coming from living in the United States. As a teacher, I have the good fortune to say the Pledge of Allegiance each and every school day. With a flag that represents so many sacrifices, there is no need for others. No greater stories of valor are as unique as those in the war to preserve the Union.

Decatur County's list of heroes includes many from the Civil War, from Colonel Ira Grover's men at Gettysburg to Wilder's Brigade and their repeating rifles. It may seem unbelievable, but at one time, Decatur County had six Medal of Honor residents. The Medal of Honor is our nation's highest military award. The Greensburg High School Student Council raised $9,000 in 2019 to erect a beautiful monument in South Park Cemetery in their honor. In fact, one of the recipients is buried nearby. Reuben Smalley fought with Benjamin Spooner's Eighty-Third Indiana Regiment. That unit fought at Vicksburg and participated in Sherman's march to the sea. I admit I am partial to the Eighty-Third, as my great-great-grandfather John Bultman served with it and was wounded twice. I'll never forget visiting Kennesaw Mountain and wondering if I was standing in the same place he once did. My daughters always said that none of our vacations were complete without a stop at a museum or a Civil War battlefield. So many stories of heroism exist from that war, but one of my favorites is that of a brave woman named Elizabeth Finnern.

Elizabeth Cain was born in Germany in 1820. She married John Finnern, and they settled in Ohio in the 1850s. After the outbreak of the Civil War, John enlisted in Company D of the Eighty-First Regiment, Ohio Volunteers. It is here that the story gets interesting. Elizabeth missed her husband so much that she enlisted as a laundress with his regiment. Her post was abolished, and she was faced with the dilemma of what to do. After she found a uniform in a storeroom, her decision was made. This brave woman fought alongside her husband. Just like everyone else, she lived on a soldier's ration and marched with a musket fifty miles a day. She participated in several noteworthy battles: Corinth, Mississippi; Pocahontas, Virginia; Huntsville, Alabama; Harrison, Missouri; Pulaski, Georgia; and Chattanooga, Fort Donelson and Shiloh, Tennessee.

At Arkansas Post, John was injured. Elizabeth then set out after his assailant and shot him. It was after this that her true identity was discovered. After three months as a soldier, she spent the next three years as a surgeon's assistant. Apparently, she was an exceptional nurse. In fact, it was at Lookout Mountain that her extraordinary services in the field hospital were noticed by General Ulysses S. Grant. He singled her out for praise and gave her a towel, a reward greatly appreciated at the time. John was mustered out in September 1864. Elizabeth had been with him the entire time. After the war, the couple bought a small farm in Laurel, Indiana. A year later, they moved to Williamstown in rural Decatur County and eventually settled in Greensburg. They were honored residents for decades, and tales of her service during the war were often shared. John died in 1905. A female doctor friend working on Elizabeth's behalf with the Women's Relief Corps successfully petitioned President Theodore Roosevelt to continue John's pension for Elizabeth. It must have been terribly difficult for her after the loss of her soulmate. Elizabeth died in 1907. The pension funds, largely unspent, were used for a beautiful Bedford stone monument placed

Elizabeth Finnern's tombstone. *Courtesy of Daniel Fayette.*

on the South Park Cemetery's Soldiers Circle. John and Elizabeth are the only married couple buried on the Soldiers Circle.

The official account of Elizabeth Finnern's story is not the one you just read. Research suggests that it is all true except the part about her dressing as a soldier and fighting alongside her husband. I take another perspective, asking the following questions: Did she march fifty miles a day alongside her husband? Yes. Did the cemetery authorities approve the request to have both John and Elizabeth Finnern buried on the Soldiers Circle? Yes. Is Elizabeth the only woman buried on the Soldiers Circle? Yes. We may never have definitive proof of her wartime service. She could not be officially listed as a soldier, as women were not accepted in the army. As an old history professor of mine used to say, "If it's not true, it should be." To John and Elizabeth Finnern, I say "thank you" for your service. Decatur County is proud of these two brave soldiers.

4

THE UNDERGROUND RAILROAD

IN DECATUR COUNTY

Growing up in Decatur County, I had heard about our local participation in the Underground Railroad. I was told of underground passageways and secret compartments. I knew that enslaved people sought freedom and followed the North Star to Canada, but that was all I knew. In college, I wrote my major history research paper on Decatur County and was amazed at the many aspects of our history that I knew nothing about. Abraham Lincoln and Bobby Kennedy each visited, and numerous communities hosted an amazing event called Chautauqua, which brought people like Helen Keller to town. But I did not come across information on Decatur County's role in the Underground Railroad. That was in 1985.

At the age of forty-three, I walked into a classroom as a teacher for the first time. As a new social studies teacher at North Decatur, I was looking for creative projects to excite my students. I had heard of an old African Methodist Episcopal Cemetery that was somewhere in the middle of a wooded area in Fugit Township. I was fortunate to find the cemetery as well as a wonderful property owner who embraced my idea of students renovating it. The cemetery had been largely untouched for 150 years. The end result was one of the most rewarding experiences of my life. The individuals buried there had been pillars of the Underground Railroad. They deserved to be honored and shown respect. Restoring the cemetery would do just that. But how did I know that the Underground Railroad had existed here? William O. Smith was the person responsible for putting together this wonderful story.

I had the good fortune to meet Bill Smith at the time of the cemetery restoration. He is our local historian and expert on the Underground Railroad. It was Bill who separated fact from legend. For that, he will always have my highest respect. I always tell my students that the legacy of Decatur County's contributions have been immense in many areas. The two that stand out are, first, our significant contributions to support the military efforts of our country, and, second, the role citizens played in the Underground Railroad. I have the highest respect for those who were willing to break the law in order to help fugitive enslaved people gain their freedom.

To understand how the local Underground Railroad operated, one needs to know a few basic facts. As fugitive slaves crossed the Ohio River, the conductors would move them northeast toward Canada. They tried to avoid undeveloped areas, which could mean treacherous travel. A hot spot for crossing was Madison, Indiana. Here, runaway enslaved people could find many conductors, due in part to a large Presbyterian population and the Presbyterian college nearby. These residents, along with Quakers, were noted abolitionists, morally opposed to slavery and willing to break the law to help the enslaved. The other advantage of Madison and Hanover's location was that each had a free Black settlement, where enslaved people could be more easily hidden during the day.

In Decatur County, the cooperation between farmers who lived in the Kingston corridor and free people of color who lived in the Snelling Settlement made for a successful partnership and resulted in a stop on the Underground Railroad. The earliest residents of Kingston, located in the eastern part of Decatur County in Fugit Township, were Presbyterian abolitionists. The majority of these people came from three families: the Donnells, the McCoys and the Hamiltons. Kingston was about fifty miles from the Kentucky border, so passengers could travel roughly twenty-five miles each night and arrive in Fugit Township in just two days. The activism of the Kingston abolitionists started early, in the 1820s. Samuel Donnell organized antislavery societies in both Kentucky and Decatur County. William Henry, another early abolitionist who settled in Decatur County, had attempted to build a "Sabbath School" for enslaved people in Kentucky, but it was closed down. He died soon after he had settled in Decatur County in 1823, leaving behind two Black children he had adopted in order to save them from a lifetime of slavery. In 1835, the first known antislavery society in Indiana was created in Kingston.

In December 1822, an African American from Nichols County, Kentucky, bought fifty-six acres of land in the northeastern part of the county in Fugit

Township. His name was Joseph Snelling, and he was the first of many people of color to successfully settle in this area near Clarksburg. It came to be known as the Snelling Settlement. By 1850, a free Black woman named Jane Speed owned eighty acres of land. This community worked hand in hand with the Kingston corridor on the Underground Railroad. The Kingston conductors would bring enslaved people to the Snelling Settlement, where they were successfully hidden during the day within the community of free Blacks. Then, by night, the journey northeast would continue. The goal of reaching Canada makes going north obvious, but some areas to the north, for instance in Indiana, were rugged country. That naturally created a northeastern path through Franklin County, reaching Canada through Detroit or via a ferry near Sandusky and Toledo.

From 1830 to 1861, the Decatur County Underground Railroad may have helped hundreds to freedom. Conductors were breaking the law, so documentation was avoided, making it difficult to know exactly how many people were helped. Still, it can be proven through five different events that at least twenty-five enslaved people were part of the Fugit Township Underground Railroad. Of the seventeen White persons documented to be conductors, fourteen are buried in the Kingston Cemetery. The only people of color specifically named were Jane Speed and Miles Meadows. The most fascinating documented case of Decatur County's participation in the Underground Railroad is that of Caroline and her four children, Frances (twelve), John (seven), Amanda (four) and Henry (two). The five of them crossed the Ohio River on the night of October 31. A man named Waggoner transported them by night to the Kingston corridor, arriving around 2:30 a.m. at the home of Angus McCoy. McCoy's son Douglas then set out with Caroline and her children in an attempt to deliver them safely to the Snelling Settlement before daylight. The attempt was unsuccessful, as the sun began to rise before they reached it. It was here that Douglas and his friend William Hamilton, whom he picked up along the way, reluctantly left them with a man of color, Pernell. They didn't know him well, and he seemed quite nervous. So William Hamilton went to get Luther Donnell to check on Caroline and her family. In the meantime, Pernell had set out with the fugitives during daylight and left them with Jane Speed. She must have been a truly amazing woman. She quickly thought to hide the family of five in an outbuilding on her property. At about this time, Woodson Clark, a White Snelling Settlement neighbor and the founder of Clarksburg, noticed unusual activity in the area. Woodson had fallen on hard times and was looking to receive the $500 reward that went with turning in fugitive slaves.

He found the family and tricked them into going with him to a "better" hiding place, a fodder house on his son's property nearby. With Caroline and her children missing, Luther Donnell and Cyrus Hamilton sprang into action. They saw to it that a writ of habeas corpus was issued, followed by a search of Woodson Clark's home. Nothing was found, but Clark was furious. It was fortunate that Caroline, obviously feeling that something wasn't right, had decided to leave the fodder house with her children, wandering alone, not knowing where to go. About this time, George Ray, the slave owner, had arrived from Kentucky. He picked up some slave hunters from Greensburg, met up with Woodson Clark and set out to find Caroline and her four young children in the Snelling Settlement. Fortunately, Caroline and her family had already been found wandering the settlement and had been hidden safely, at least for the moment.

It was at this point in the story that Luther Donnell and William Hamilton devised a plan to elude George Ray and his gang. The children were separated, with the two older children transported during the day with an African American couple and their family to the home of a conductor in Union County, William Beard. That night, Black operatives separated

AME Cemetery connected with Decatur County's Underground Railroad. *Author collection.*

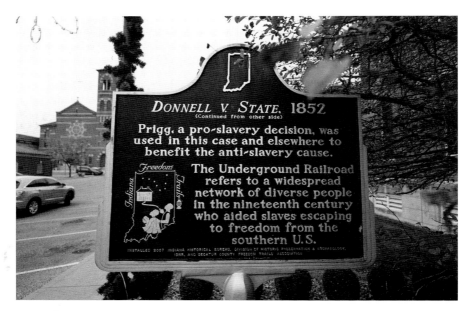

Luther Donnell Monument. *Courtesy of Daniel Fayette.*

Caroline from her youngest children. Dressed as a man, Caroline rode by wagon through the night with Donnell and Hamilton, arriving at the home of Thomas Donnell, where she was reunited with her two youngest children. The next day, the three hid at Thomas's home. At nightfall, Luther Donnell and William Hamilton took the three of them by carriage to the home of William Beard, where the family of five rejoiced in their reunion. Caroline and her children proceeded northeast along the Underground Railroad. I am pleased to say that they made it safely to freedom in Canada. This was documented by a thank-you letter written by Caroline to Luther Donnell. While this story reads like an amazing adventure, it was a life-or-death situation for Caroline and her family and a risk for the White families in the Kingston area who helped them. It is truly awe-inspiring to think these events took place in Decatur County.

Postscript: Luther Donnell was prosecuted for his role in aiding Caroline and her family, who were considered property and fugitive slaves. No one else was charged. Donnell was convicted, but on appeal, the conviction was overturned and set aside by the Indiana Supreme Court. The slave owner, George Ray, won a civil lawsuit against Donnell and Hamilton for the amount of $2,500 for the loss of his "property." Antislavery activists helped the two pay the judgment.

JANET RUMSEY

ALL-STAR WITH THE ALL-AMERICAN GIRLS PROFESSIONAL BASEBALL LEAGUE

ach year, I love to teach my students about World War II—the battles, the heroes, the Holocaust and so much more. I also make sure they know the story of the All-American Girls Professional Baseball League and one of its greatest players, Burney's own Janet Rumsey.

In 1943, Philip Wrigley and a small group of Major League Baseball owners launched the first and only professional baseball league for women, the All-American Girls Professional Baseball League. The owners feared that Major League Baseball could be forced to shut down, as much of the league's top talent, like Joe DiMaggio, was fighting in the war. It amazes me to this day to learn how many of our country's athletes and celebrities saw combat. In fact, the most decorated American soldier was future movie star Audie Murphy. Another challenge for MLB was gas rationing. In the spring of 1943, tryouts were held at Wrigley Field, and a new league was created.

The league ran from 1943 to 1954, and the teams were based in the Midwest. The most successful team was the Rockford Peaches. They were the team depicted in the classic Penny Marshall film *A League of Their Own*. The movie, featuring stars like Madonna, Geena Davis and Tom Hanks, brought national attention to this nearly forgotten treasure of American history. The movie was filmed in Indiana, and the filming locations make for a good reason to "wander" the state. The Rockford Peaches home games were filmed in Huntingburg, using the same stadium as the one used for the movie *Eight Men Out*. The visitors' games were played in Evansville, home to today's minor-league team the Evansville Otters. It is one of the oldest ballparks in America. If you go there today, you can see the *R* logos for the other team featured in the movie, the Racine Belles. Indiana was well represented in the All-American Girls Professional Baseball League, with two successful teams, the Fort Wayne Daisies and the team Janet Rumsey would star for, the South Bend Blue Sox.

Janet was born in Moores Hill on October 16, 1931. She was the daughter of Lawrence and Mabel Rumsey. Janet learned to play the game at an early age, even playing on the junior high boys' team. She graduated from Burney High School in 1949. The following year, she saw a short film on the Fort Wayne Daisies, so she wrote to them and asked for a tryout. She did not make the team. Refusing to give up, she secured a spot on the 1951 Blue Sox. She originally tried out at first base and the outfield, but Coach Karl Winsch saw she had a great arm, thus beginning her stellar career as a hurler.

Janet threw and batted right-handed and was pitching in 1951 for the powerful South Bend Blue Sox. She pitched part of the season for Battle Creek in an effort to keep the team afloat. She ended 1951 with the Blue Sox

Janet Rumsey. *Courtesy of Decatur County Historical Society.*

and helped them win the league championship. She ended her first year with a 4-8 record and an impressive ERA of 2.52. In 1952, she was the Blue's go-to ace, leading the team in seeing action in 26 games. That year, the Blue Sox faced the famed Rockford Peaches in the best-of-five championship series. By now, Janet's repertoire of pitches included a hard fastball, a sinker and a sidearm curve. The team was leading two games to one in the series, and the eyes of all Blue Sox fans were on the starter, Burney's own Janet Rumsey. The game was a classic pitchers' duel, with Janet throwing a 10-inning complete game that the Sox won in a thriller, 2–1. The Blue Sox went on to win the series securing their second league championship. Janet finished the season with a 9-10 record and a 2.33 ERA. The 1953 season was a struggle for Blue Sox fans, but Janet still posted an 11-19 record and a 2.42 ERA and finished second in the league in innings pitched (249), third in shutouts (4) and seventh in strikeouts (86).

It would be 1954 that showed Janet Rumsey at her best. In a season noted for hitting—the league moved to a smaller, more lively ball—Janet posted a mark of 15-6, finishing second in the league in wins and second in shutouts (6) and innings pitched (181). She led the league with a 2.16 ERA and tied for the most complete games (21). These accomplishments would lead to Janet's selection to the 1954 All-Star team. She also has the distinction of throwing the last no-hitter in the history of the league. The league ended soon after, but that does not diminish the impressive career of Janet Rumsey.

6

CARL FISHER

Carl Graham Fisher was born on January 12, 1874, in Greensburg, Indiana. He was the son of Albert and Ida Fisher. Albert, an attorney, was said to be prone to drinking too much, and he left the family when Carl was only twelve. Carl suffered from a severe undetected astigmatism, which led to struggles in the classroom. He dropped out of school and began working at an early age. Carl's entrepreneurial spirit was said to have shown itself early on, as he was known to sell advertising on his sled as he went speeding down the biggest hill in town. Fisher's mother moved the family to Indianapolis when Carl was fourteen. By the age of seventeen, he and his brother had opened a bicycle repair shop. This business greatly expanded when they started selling bicycles, and Carl's promotional genius began to show itself. His antics in promoting his business became legendary, including riding a bike on a wire that connected two downtown buildings. At this time, a new mode of transportation emerged, one that Carl would embrace and become famous for: the automobile.

Carl opened what is thought to be the first automobile dealership in the United States in Indianapolis. He and James Allison invented the first acetylene headlight, and their factories supplied the nation's cars. He sold his interests to Union Carbide in 1913, giving him time to work on what he really loved: automobile racing. In 1909, he was the principal developer of the Indianapolis Motor Speedway, and after improvements, including the laying of 3.2 million paving bricks, the first Indianapolis 500 was held on Memorial Day, May 30, 1911, as eighty thousand spectators watched.

CARL FISHER
(Continued from other side)

Proponent of the Good Roads Movement to expand and improve the nation's road networks. Fisher advocated construction of U.S. transcontinental roads including east-west Lincoln Highway (1912) and north-south Dixie Highway (1914). Such roads enabled long-distance travel by automobile. He also developed Miami Beach into major resort destination. Died July 15, 1939.

INSTALLED 2014 INDIANA HISTORICAL BUREAU, GOGREENSBURG, AND THE CITY OF GREENSBURG

Above: Carl Fisher Monument. *Courtesy of Daniel Fayette.*

Right: Carl Fisher. *Courtesy of Daniel Fayette.*

Carl Fisher's accomplishments were many by 1911, but many more were to come. In 1913, he developed the first east–west highway, the Lincoln Highway, which connected New York City to San Francisco. He then developed the first southern highway, the Dixie Highway, which opened in September 1916. With a clear route now, he changed Miami Beach from a swamp to a gorgeous beachside destination. This was followed by the development of Montauk, Long Island.

Sadly, the Great Depression was not kind to Carl Fisher. By 1926, his estimated worth was $100 million. But he lost most of it due to the stock market crash. His seventeen-year marriage ended in divorce, and he died on July 15, 1939, of a gastric hemorrhage while living in Miami. Fisher was sixty-five years old and is buried at Crown Hill Cemetery in Indianapolis.

Few Hoosiers have left such a lasting legacy. In the typical Indiana way, he promoted his projects but not himself. There is no Fisher Highway or Fisher 500. From beginning the "Greatest Spectacle in Racing" to creating our first paved highways, which opened up travel for millions of Americans, the name Carl Fisher should be admired and respected.

7

PAUL AND JACK SHRIVER

I remember growing up in the 1960s and '70s and my dad taking me to the high school football and basketball games. Prior to the fall of 1971, when the new high school was opened, I recall seeing the Pirates play on South Ireland Street. The one thing I remember most was the impressive scoreboard with all its lights, and at the top of the sign in big letters were the words *Shriver Field*. I always knew it honored two brothers who died during World War II, but that was about all I knew. Over time, I learned more about the story of the Shriver brothers. It goes something like this.

Paul Sanders Shriver was the older of the two brothers, sons of John and Ruth. They also had four sisters. Paul graduated from Greensburg High School in 1930. "Petie," as he was called, was a member of the Greensburg YMCA's famous men's volleyball team. The team, led by big Ed Doerflinger, not only won the state title but also won a world tournament in the 1930s in Houston. A nice picture of the team is in the conference room of the Greensburg YMCA today. My namesake, John William Goddard, was on the team as well. Paul enlisted in the U.S. Army Air Corps and achieved the rank of sergeant. He was a tail gunner on a B-24 Liberator bomber in the Pacific. On December 26, 1942, his plane was engaged in an aerial fight off the coast of Australia and crashed. There were no survivors. Paul was twenty-nine years old.

Jack Graham Shriver was five years younger than Paul. Jack also served in the air corps, flying planes in the Pacific and achieving the rank of first lieutenant. He survived the attack of December 7, 1941, at Pearl Harbor. It was in Honolulu that he met and married his wife, Holly. Jack flew B-17s in the Pacific. He was in over sixteen battles, from Midway and Guadalcanal to the Solomon and Wake Islands. He flew over 750 combat hours. Once, his plane sank a Japanese destroyer. On another occasion, his plane was forced to make an emergency landing, and several crewmen were killed by enemy fire. Jack survived, but he contracted malaria and was reassigned to Pratt Air Force Base in Pratt, Kansas. There, he trained rookie pilots on the new B-26 Marauders. On September 23, 1943, Jack was aboard a routine forty-five-minute training flight when the weather took a turn for the worse as the B-26 approached Pratt. Just then, the left engine blew. The plane was flying too low for parachute deployment and was headed right for the local school. Eyewitnesses confirmed that it was Jack steering the plane away from the school and town before it crashed into a vacant hillside. All three crew members were killed. Jack Shriver was survived by his wife and his son Jack Jr., born after his father's death.

Rod Dyerly was a seventh-grader in Pratt, Kansas, and was an eyewitness to the heroism of Lieutenant Shriver as he guided the plane away from the school. Dyerly would also serve in the military and retired with the rank of major. He made it his mission to honor the memory of Jack Shriver and his heroism. In 2006, he enlisted the aid of Indiana senator Richard Lugar.

Shriver Field. *Courtesy of Daniel Fayette.*

Ultimately, Shriver was awarded the Air Force Award of Valor. Major Dyerly later wrote a book, *The Final Flight of a B-26 Bomber*. He visited Greensburg and in a special ceremony gave copies of the book to the school and public library, several World War II veterans and Jack's widow, Holly. Each fall, hundreds of players and fans enter Shriver Field. How it got its name should never be forgotten.

Jack and Paul's sister Virginia enlisted in the air corps after her brothers' deaths and served in Washington, D.C. She married Gilman Stewart, a decorated World War II pilot who flew thirty-five combat missions in Europe.

8

FRED CRAIG

ANIMATOR EXTRAORDINAIRE

I will never forget the pre-Chautauqua dinner I was hosting when iconic *Greensburg Daily News* columnist Pat Smith introduced me to her friend Fred Craig. I met an incredibly nice man who went on to tell me about his career working in animation and filmmaking. When he asked if I had heard of some of the films he had worked on, like *An American Tail* and *Rock-A-Doodle*, I was blown away. My daughters loved those films growing up, and I quickly understood I was meeting a living legend.

One of my activities at Greensburg High School is sitting on its Hall of Fame selection committee. When Fred Craig's name was brought up, he was a unanimous choice, and this allowed me to get to know him better. Fred was a graduate of the class of 1960, and I was fascinated to learn that he began making films in his teens and was self-taught. His first commissioned work was as a seventeen-year-old completing a seventy-two-minute film, *The Greensburg Story*, about the city's 1959 centennial. Fred enlisted in the military after high school and, following his four years of service, moved to Los Angeles to pursue his dream of filmmaking.

His training came from some of the best, like Jerry Lewis and Chuck Jones. He developed his skills in animation and filmmaking working for Hanna-Barbera as a filmmaker, producer, creative director, artist and writer. He created his independent production company, Fred Craig Production Inc., which brought opportunities to work with industry giants like Disney, Paramount, Universal and MGM. It was during this period that Fred

Fred Craig. *Courtesy of April Marinoff.*

worked on a variety of animation and live-action projects, even working on thirty episodes of *Sesame Street*. I once hosted a wonderful blues artist as part of a Chautauqua, Mac Arnold, best known for playing with the great Muddy Waters. Fred and Mac were actually connected through their work on the 1970s television show *Soul Train*. Fred was everywhere and working with many people during this time.

It was in 1979 that Fred met with Disney animators/producers Gary Goldman and Don Bluth, and he accepted their invitation to join the brand-new Don Bluth Studios as a production management executive and technical director. From Los Angeles, they headed for Sullivan-Bluth Studios in Ireland. It was during this period that Fred played an integral part in creating iconic animated family films that are still enjoyed and treasured today and will be for many years to come. I remember that first night I met Fred. When he talked about Don Bluth, I was star struck. My oldest daughter, Clare, and I absolutely loved all of those films!

Fievel the mouse and the award-winning song *Somewhere Out There* from *An American Tail* was probably his best-known work. Fred said he always had a special affinity for *The Secret of NIMH*; the Pratt household always had a special affinity for *Rock-A-Doodle*. I never would have imagined that one of the key animators/director of that film and many others was a Greensburg

High School graduate. Fred worked on numerous other well-known films, like *The Land Before Time* and *Thumbelina*.

Fred retired to his hometown of Greensburg, and for those of us who had the good fortune to get to know him, we will be forever blessed. Fred played an active role in Art on the Square, which often showed his photography. Sadly, Fred died in 2020, but the legacy of his films will continue to bring smiles and happiness to children of all ages for years to come.

9

OSCAR EWING

FATHER OF MEDICARE

*W*ill Cumback must be regarded as the most noted statesman of the nineteenth century from Decatur County. Without hesitation, I would argue that Oscar Ewing was Decatur County's greatest statesman of the twentieth century. Ewing, known as the father of Medicare, was born on March 8, 1889, in Greensburg. The 1906 Greensburg High School graduate received his bachelor's degree from Indiana University and his law degree from Harvard. He was a captain in the U.S. Army during World War I. After the war, he began practicing law in New York City and in 1937 was a cofounder of the firm Hughes, Hubbard and Ewing. The Hughes was Charles Evan Hughes, chief justice of the U.S. Supreme Court. The address was 1 Wall Street.

Oscar Ross Ewing, Jack to his friends, was a lifelong Democrat. In 1940, he became the assistant chairman of the Democratic National Committee and moved up to vice-chairman in 1942. In 1947, President Harry Truman appointed him Federal Security Administrator, and it was in that capacity that over the next five years his work would leave a legacy for future generations. Oscar was one of the chief architects of the Fair Deal, which helped President Truman get reelected in an upset over Thomas Dewey.

The boldest element of the Fair Deal was the implementation of a national health insurance program that would be funded by payroll taxes. It was as controversial then as it is now. The highest priority of the plan was health insurance for the elderly. These bold ideas were derailed by the Korean War. Truman's popularity tumbled, and he chose not to run again.

Oscar Ewing (*third from left*). *Courtesy of Harry S. Truman Presidential Library.*

When the Democratic nominee for president, Adlai Stevenson, lost in 1952, that was the end of the Fair Deal and its ideals, at least for the time being. But in 1966, President Lyndon Johnson resurrected the idea of Medicare as a part of his Great Society platform. When Congress passed Medicare, LBJ chose the Truman Library as the site for the signing ceremony. Joining the president on Air Force One was none other than the man referred to as the father of Medicare, Oscar Ross Ewing.

It should be noted that Ewing, as Truman's federal security administrator, had many other accomplishments. He played a critical role in civil rights, advising Truman to desegregate the military. Ewing was seriously criticized for following the recommendation of the American Dental Association to add small amounts of fluoride to the water supply to improve the health of Americans' teeth. When Truman was wavering about recognizing the new state of Israel, Ewing weighed in again and encouraged him to do so. The United States was the first country to recognize its official existence.

The greats of Decatur County have had love and respect for their roots, and none were born with silver spoons in their mouths. That is certainly true of Oscar Ewing. He created scholarships for Greensburg and Indiana

University students that still exist today. After he graduated from IU, he and his sister sold subscriptions to the magazine the *Saturday Evening Post* to help pay for his tuition to Harvard Law School. Their mission was to be educated and be successful. Oscar Ewing certainly fulfilled that mission and left a legacy that should be admired.

10

THE HOOSIER SCHOOLMASTER

AN INDIANA CLASSIC SET IN MILFORD

*H*ave you read the J. Edward Eggleston novel *The Hoosier Schoolmaster*? Since I first became acquainted with the book some thirty-five years ago, I have known only one other person who read it. As wonderful as our local library is, even it no longer has a copy. To summarize, the book was a bestseller in 1871 that sold millions of copies and whose influence can still be felt today. Furthermore, the novel is based on real people and events in rural western Decatur County near the Flat Rock River. This is the story of *The Hoosier Schoolmaster*.

The Eggleston children grew up in Vevay in a happy, well-read home. The family of six met with tragedy in 1848, when J. Edward's father, a successful local attorney, died unexpectedly. Urged by his mother's family, they moved to Milford in western Decatur County in 1851.

The Hoosier Schoolmaster would be published to the delight of millions twenty years later. The author drew on the real people he met and the experiences he had in 1851 and 1852 in Milford. His mother remarried, to a Methodist minister, and the family moved to New Albany, Indiana. J. Edward and his brother George both became rural Indiana schoolmasters before moving to New York City, where they became successful writers. But it was *The Hoosier Schoolmaster* that made the name *Eggleston* known throughout the country.

The plot begins simply enough, as a new schoolmaster from the big town in the county embarks on the adventure of moving to a rural, somewhat

The Hoosier Schoolmaster spelling match. *Public domain.*

backward part of the county in the early 1850s. Decatur County received its first modern settlers in 1819 and was officially incorporated in 1822.

The novel is to be enjoyed by everyone, but without giving it away, I will entice you with a few of the highlights. The young schoolmaster is Ralph Hartsook, who must quickly create positive relationships in a challenging setting, a one-room schoolhouse. What ensues is great character development, from his unlikely good friend Bud to an unexpected love interest. The setting is the backwoods of Indiana, outside of the Flat Rock River in Milford. Part of the charm is Eggleston's use of the regional dialect. Do not let that intimidate you, as it is very easy to follow. It was said that Eggleston's use of the dialect influenced Mark Twain's *Tom Sawyer* and *Huckleberry Finn*.

The book set off a trend of great Hoosier authors and poets, from Gene Stratton-Porter and James Whitcomb Riley to Booth Tarkington and Theodore Dreiser, among many others. Hoosier authors were known for great romances, and Eggleston does not disappoint. It is not a major shock who it involves, but you will be truly delighted. The plot even delves into social justice issues and was referred to as the *Nicholas Nickleby* of its time.

I love the fact that one of the funniest aspects of the book is the spelling contest. In fact, the book set off a spelling bee craze. The *Greensburg Daily News* wrote of the Greensburg claim in 1874 that the town hosted the first community spelling bee. Such a unique contribution to history should be appreciated by the good folks at Scripps-Howard. The book also features a mystery, a robbery and a romance, all based on actual events.

Today, we often see tourists marveling at the Tree on the Courthouse Tower, but it is amazing to think that people from far and wide once made the pilgrimage to Milford to see the actual sites of J. Edward Eggleston and *The Hoosier Schoolmaster*. Hollywood came calling in 1924 and made a silent move of the bestseller. In 1935, a talkie film was made. Its popularity led to the 1937 film *The Hoosier Schoolboy* starring Mickey Rooney. It, too, was based on Eggleston's book and was set in Decatur County. The book is available for purchase from online booksellers; it is also in the public domain and can be accessed online. It's a great read!

11

GREENSBURG

HOW WE GOT OUR NAME

*P*ick any town and then pay attention to its name and street names to make a connection with its history. Greensburg is a good example. When I grew up here, we lived in two homes, one on Washington and the other on Lincoln. Those are certainly iconic names. Not too far from those streets is Hendricks Street, named after the founder of Greensburg. When the founding fathers of our community met to name the county, they looked no further than the great naval hero Stephen Decatur. The brave seaman will forever be known as one of the remarkable leaders of the War of 1812, but my favorite story is how he fought the Barbary pirates in 1803. Teaching history for the Greensburg Pirates in the County of Decatur, my students must learn of this act of heroism. I like to begin my lesson by singing a few bars of "The Marines' Hymn," "From the halls of Montezuma, to the shores of Tripoli." I'm no Jim Nabors, but it expresses how Stephen Decatur faced the Barbary pirates in 1803.

The pirates of Tripoli had been attacking American ships and kidnapping their crews. Decatur and his ship, the *Intrepid*, were nearing the *Philadelphia*, an American ship seized by the pirates and in the harbor at Tripoli. Decatur's men snuck aboard in the dead of night. When Stephen Decatur stood up, the Americans attacked. The pirates lost twenty men, but not one of Decatur's crew was lost or injured. As the Americans could not tow the *Philadelphia* out of the harbor, the ship was set ablaze, making it useless to the pirates. Stephen Decatur was the last to leave the ship. Horatio Nelson

Sarah Hendricks, daughter of Thomas and Elizabeth Hendricks. *Courtesy of Daniel Fayette.*

referred to this as a true act of bravery. Sadly, Decatur was killed in a dual in 1820 at the age of forty-one.

Nathanael Greene, for whom the town of Greensburg was named, was quite the hero himself, known as the second-greatest general of the Continental army. He was the commander of the southern campaign, and his outnumbered troops successfully engaged in guerrilla warfare. This led to victories at places like Germantown, Monmouth and Trenton. His tactics prevented Charles, Lord Cornwallis from invading North Carolina and Virginia.

Great bravery and heroism is represented in our community's names, but the reason behind the naming of Greensburg, Indiana, may be more about romance than history. Thomas Hendricks was the founder of Greensburg. He was the brother of an Indiana governor and the uncle of a future vice president. Still, it was his wife, Elizabeth, who is said to have had the greatest influence on the naming of our town. Elizabeth missed her home in Greensburg, Pennsylvania, a small town thirty miles from Pittsburgh, and she wanted her new home to be named after her old one. She suggested there should be a vote among the men to determine the name. That's when things got interesting. The new community had a much higher number of eligible young men compared to women. Elizabeth and Thomas Hendricks had five daughters, all single and of an age suitable for courting. Elizabeth let it be known that she would look favorably upon the young men who voted for Greensburg to be the name of the new town. Seventeen young men voted for Greensburg, making it the resounding winner. Three of the seventeen would later be her sons-in-law. Greensburg is a fine name, and we have Elizabeth Hendricks to thank for it.

12

NORMAN SELBY

AKA KID McCoy

*I*t has probably been thirty years since I watched a boxing match on television. We always watched the main events on TV growing up, so I was well acquainted with the legends of the sport. Boxing movies have become more iconic than the sport itself, from *Rocky* and *Cinderella Man* to *Raging Bull* and *The Champ*. Still, I was fascinated to read a 1959 *Greensburg Daily News* article that introduced me to Kid McCoy and his local connections. If ever a real-life person exemplified Dr. Jekyll and Mr. Hyde, it was McCoy.

Norman Selby was born on October 13, 1872, in the small Rush County community of Moscow. He was the son of Francis and Emily Selby. By all accounts, Norman grew up getting into fights, and he enjoyed hopping on freight cars to Cincinnati. According to the newspaper, a couple of interesting facts emerged, which is what caught my eye and made me want to include his story here. First were the differing accounts of how he got his boxing name. The conventional story was that, at the age of eighteen, he became a professional boxer and was looking for a ringside name. He took a name from a burlesque act featuring the exploits of safecrackers Kid McCoy and Spike Hennessey. The local story is quite different. As a teenager, Norman once ran away from home. The authorities caught up with him in Decatur County. When they asked him his name, he looked around and noticed he was standing near a sign that read "McCoy Station," so he replied, "Frank McCoy," and the name stuck. The second noteworthy item from the *Greensburg Daily News* article was that for a winter he lived in Greensburg on Broadway Street.

Boxing was extremely popular in the United States, and boxers themselves were as popular as any basketball or football superstars of today. Baseball was just emerging as America's pastime. Kid McCoy took the ring by storm, winning his first twenty bouts, mostly by knockout. To this day, he is famous for the development of a particular punch, a corkscrew punch that is similar to a left hook, with a twist at the end.

Most accounts attribute the saying "the real McCoy" to Kid McCoy. One account suggests that he would fake an illness before suddenly "recovering" and defeating his opponent, causing some to wonder, "Is this the real McCoy?" Another version has Kid in a saloon tussle with a drunk. Kid told him, "Beat it, I'm Kid McCoy!" The drunk came back with, "If you're Kid McCoy, then I'm George Washington." The Kid then popped him in the jaw, and the drunk fell to the ground. When he woke, he was reported to have said, "Jeez, that was the real McCoy."

Kid McCoy was by no means a large man, standing five feet, eleven inches and weighing 160 pounds. He was known for winning a title then continuing to move up a class. The slender boxer eventually fought in the heavyweight division. In March 1896, he defeated Tommy Ryan to win the world welterweight title. In December 1897, Kid won the world middleweight title with a fifteenth-round knockout of Dan Creeden. McCoy went on to the heavyweight division and defeated the likes of Peter Maher and Gus Ruhlin but was defeated by "Gentleman Jim" Corbett. In his last bout, he defeated British petty officer Matthew Curron in London in 1914. His impressive career record was 160 wins and 6 losses.

After service to his country, Kid McCoy landed in Hollywood, where he made celebrity friends. Kid made appearances in eleven silent films, thanks in part to his friendship with director D.W. Griffith. He even taught another friend, Charlie Chaplin, how to box in a film. His family in Moscow followed him west; unfortunately, the rest of the story has its ups and downs.

Kid's investments in an auto dealership and jewelry store failed. He married nine times, three times to the same woman. Many of his boxing matches were clouded with his antics in order to win, such as faking illness and announcing he was not training. His bout with Corbett was rumored to be staged. Nearly broke and drinking too much, at the age of thirty, McCoy began seeing Theresa Mors, the wealthy wife of an antiques dealer. The two began arguing, and one morning, Theresa was found dead in her apartment, killed by a shot to the head. The next day, Kid went to Mors's antique shop in an apparent robbery attempt. He held twelve people hostage before being apprehended by the police. McCoy was tried for murder but convicted of

Kid McCoy (*left*). *Public domain.*

manslaughter and sent to San Quentin. Kid McCoy always claimed that Theresa Mors killed herself.

In prison, Kid was known as a good inmate and was respected. Once, while serving on an outside detail, the prison work crew was witness to a small-engine airplane crash near them. Kid dashed in and saved the life of the pilot. Kid was promoted in prison to fire chief, a role in which he excelled. His visitors at this time included Lionel Barrymore and Al Jolson. He wasn't eligible for an early release, as he did not have a job waiting for him. Henry Ford heard this and agreed to hire McCoy as an athletic trainer. McCoy married again and led a largely unassuming life in Michigan. He once saved the lives of four people whose boat had capsized. On April 18, 1940, Kid McCoy took his own life by an overdose of sleeping pills. He had earned almost $300,000 in prize money during his career but died with less than $20 on him. Kid McCoy was a fascinating, complicated, tragic character whose story deserves greater research. Although primarily a Rush Countian, his local ties should not be forgotten.

13

FAVORITE SOLDIER STORIES

Civil War

In my research for this book, I found the number of soldiers from Decatur County and their heroism simply boggled my mind. Heroism is especially evident in those who served from Decatur County during the Civil War. In the history of the county, we have had six men in the military receive the Medal of Honor, the highest distinction awarded for military valor. All six served during the Civil War. They are:

1. Marion T. Anderson (1839–1904), captain, Company D, Fifty-First Indiana Infantry, Nashville, Tennessee, 12/16/1864 (date of action)
2. James Dunlavy (1844–1923), private, Company D, Third Iowa Cavalry, Osage, Kansas, 10/25/1864
3. Louis J. Bruner (1834–1912), private, Company H, Fifth Indiana Cavalry, Walker's Ford, Tennessee, 12/2/1863
4. John N. Opel (1843–1925), private, Company C, Seventh Indiana Cavalry, The Wilderness, Virginia, 5/5/1865
5. Jacob H. Overturf (1842–1900), private, Company K, Eighty-Third Indiana Infantry, Vicksburg, Mississippi, 5/22/1863
6. Reuben Smalley (1839–1926), private, Company F, Eighty-Third Indiana Infantry, Vicksburg, Mississippi, 5/22/1863

Medal of Honor Monument. *Author collection.*

Reuben Smalley. *Courtesy of Daniel Fayette.*

Indiana history and the Civil War have always held the intrigue of that raid in the summer of 1863, when General John Hunt Morgan struck fear and terror into Hoosiers as his soldiers raided southern Indiana, in communities from Corydon and Salem to Vernon and Versailles. They ransomed Corydon for cash and supplies, burned a railroad bridge in Vernon, burned the town of Dupont's storehouse and stole two thousand smoked hams. Men on both sides died at the Battle of Corydon. In Salem, they looted stores and stole $500. Scouts entered Decatur County, and all available men were assembled at the courthouse. But after raiding Versailles, Morgan's troops went northeast into Ohio. On July 24, 1862, a Decatur Countian, First Lieutenant Robert Braden of the Seventh Indiana, Company D, was killed by Morgan's Raiders near Henderson, Kentucky. As stated, Morgan's men inflicted real damage in this part of Indiana and should never be glorified.

If I was told I could go back in time to any date in Decatur County history, it would definitely be February 12, 1861, the day Abraham Lincoln came to town. His words were few, but as he left, he told the band to play on. The Greensburg Brass Band was playing a rousing rendition of "Hail, Columbia." It would be only a few short months later that many of these men would volunteer to play on the front lines as part of the Greensburg Regimental Band. George Rhiver was one such man. In fact, at the time of his enlistment, he was the owner of the *Decatur Republican*. He was killed in action on April 21, 1862, at the age of twenty-one.

WORLD WAR I

St. Paul resident, Private First Class William Baxter, Machine Gun Company, Sixteenth Infantry, First Division, received the Silver Star for exceptional bravery on May 28, 1918, during the capture and defense of Cantigny under heavy enemy fire. He broke up fire attacks before being killed in action.

On September 12, 1918, Sergeant Carl Joseph AmRhein, Company G, Ninth Infantry, Second Division, and Sergeant Frank Dullaghan received the Silver Star for fearlessly rushing machine-gun nests under heavy fire.

One of the greatest events that I ever had the honor of hosting was a special commemoration marking our country's one-hundredth anniversary of entry into World War I. As part of that program, community members decorated the graves of all the local soldiers who died in the service of our country. Four of them are buried in American cemeteries in Europe.

Left: Joseph Kinker.
Author collection.

Below: Soldiers Circle.
Courtesy of Daniel Fayette.

We reached out to those cemeteries and were able to get each grave site decorated. One of those soldiers was Joseph Kinker.

Private Joseph Henry Kinker of New Point was born on August 1, 1893. While serving our country in France during World War I, like so many of our soldiers and citizens, he died of pneumonia on September 19, 1918. He is buried at Oise-Aisne at the American Cemetery and Memorial in France.

WORLD WAR II

The first time I walked into a classroom as a history teacher, I was forty-three years old. My eyes were soon opened to the lack of prior knowledge of history that high school students have. As a U.S. history teacher to high school juniors, I have found that the vast majority have no idea when Pearl Harbor occurred. Many have never even heard of it. When I have the opportunity to relate a personal or local story, it adds to their retaining the information and motivates them to want to learn more.

I had the good fortune to visit the USS *Arizona*, where a fresh quart of oil continues to rise to the surface from the wreck every day. Speaking of everyday occurrences, it is rare I don't drive by American Legion Post no. 129 and see the sign reading "Welsh, Crawley, Kramer," for whom the post is named. Joseph Welsh was the first Decatur Countian killed during World War I. Wallace DeWitt Crawley attended Clarksburg High School and enlisted in the navy on his eighteenth birthday. He, too, died on the *Arizona* on December 7, 1941. Robert Rudolf Kramer, gunner second class, was a 1938 graduate of New Point High School. He died aboard the USS *Arizona* when the Japanese attacked Pearl Harbor. His body was one of the few recovered, and he is buried at the National Memorial Cemetery of the Pacific in Hawaii. Their names are rightfully honored by American Legion Post no. 129.

I will never forget the day about nine years ago when one of my students, Stephanie Bruns, told me a very interesting story about her grandfather. Paul Geis was born and raised in the Enochsburg area. He served in the U.S. Air Force during World War II, from January 14, 1943, to November 5, 1945. His plane went down in Amsterdam on March 22, 1944. There was an eyewitness to Paul's parachute coming down under enemy fire: Anne Frank. I went to the building where the Frank family hid, and it was one of the most memorable and moving sites I have ever visited. My students have interviewed Anne's good friend Hannah Pick-Gosler on several occasions.

Stephanie's story about her grandfather brought added meaning to Decatur County's role in World War II. On Thursday, March 22, 1944, Anne wrote in her diary,

> *Dear Kitty,*
> *A plane crashed near here yesterday; the occupants were able to jump out in time by parachute. The machine crashed onto a school, but there were no children there at the time. The result was a small fire and two people killed. The Germans shot at the airmen terribly as they were coming down. The Amsterdammers who saw it nearly exploded with rage and indignation at the cowardliness of such a deed. We—I'm speaking of the ladies—nearly jumped out of our skins. I loathe the blasted shooting.*

Paul J. Geis was a prisoner of war for fourteen months. After the war, he came back to Decatur County, where he worked for the telephone company in Greensburg, retiring after thirty-six years. He was also a self-employed farmer. He married Margaret Hodapp, and they had two children, Phillip and Mary. He died on June 14, 2001, at the age of seventy-eight.

Kathryn Ernstes Baily was a 1932 Greensburg High School graduate who became a very skilled nurse. She enlisted in the U.S. Army Nurse Corps on June 8, 1942, and rose to the rank of captain. On D-Day, June 6, 1944, she was in charge of one thousand beds during the Normandy invasion. What follows is an excerpt from her diary account of that historic day:

> *6 June, 1944*
> *At 6 a.m. I awakened to the ominous sound of plane after plane passing overhead—had heard them all through the night, in fact, and at seven a.m. we got the news broadcast that the continent had been invaded-D-Day!*
> *Our feelings are a bit scrambled at this point—a sense of relief mingles with dread and apprehension for what our men are going into.*
> *Meantime, we wait, and "train," and hope, and pray.*

VIETNAM WAR

It has been a challenge to choose just a few of our brave soldiers to highlight, particularly from the Vietnam War. I was born in 1963; as a youngster, I remember seeing the reports of the war and our troops who died. I think that, for many, the scenes of the war will be forever entrenched in their minds.

Ricky Alan Pate

Can you imagine being in Vietnam during the war as an eighteen-year-old? That was where PFC Ricky Alan Pate found himself. On October 13, 1971, he was a crew member aboard a U.S. Army helicopter. Other crew members were pilots Chief Warrant Officer 2 Ronald K. Schulz and Warrant Officer 1 John S. Chrin, crew chief SP4 Michael L. Darrah and medic Sergeant Hugo A. Gaytan. Their job that night, as it was most every night, was to undertake a medivac mission to save the sick and wounded. The flight took place in monsoon rains in the Seven Sister Mountains along the Cambodian border near Chow Doc. The pilot reported that they had to fly primarily by using their instruments because of the weather. Radar contact was lost when the helicopter was about seven miles from a two-thousand-foot mountain. The aircraft crashed into the mountain near Chau Lang, Republic of Vietnam. There were no survivors. The bodies were recovered the following morning. Ricky Alan Pate was just eighteen years old.

Another section of this book remembers a great day in local history, May 3, 1968, when Senator Robert Kennedy came to town. One memory struck me in particular, from a very treasured citizen and family friend, Phyllis Hellmich. Her family's welcoming house was a second home in my childhood. She said about Kennedy's visit: "I was privileged to be invited with a group of women to meet Bobby Kennedy at Keillor's after he arrived. I have never shook such soft hands. Mr. Kennedy was very kind and gentle to Lucy Shutters when she talked to him about her son, Pat, they lost in the war."

Patrick Alan Shutters was born on December 3, 1946. When I found out he had graduated from Greensburg High School in 1964, I went to the library to see a copy of that year's *Tower Tree* yearbook. His senior picture shows a young man with a million-dollar smile. Looking at the picture, I thought this must have been a student active in clubs and teams, maximizing his youthful experiences and bringing joy to those around him. The yearbook says he was a member of the Booster Club, Breeze Staff, Annual Staff, FBLA, Chorus, Hi-Y, 6-Men Concessions, Pep Club and Follies, and that he was prom chairman and played football, basketball and track. First Lieutenant Patrick Alan Shutters, twenty-one, was a recipient of the Silver and Bronze Star. He was the first person from Greensburg killed in Vietnam, on March 15, 1968.

Growing up in the Pratt household, we loved sports, Westerns and war movies. We were instilled with a love and respect for our country and those who sacrificed everything, like the men I have written about here. Their stories should always be remembered and honored.

14

THE OREGON TRAIL AND ITS
DECATUR COUNTY CONNECTION

*T*he Oregon Trail has always fascinated me, as it has many other Americans. Had I lived then, I too might have heeded Thomas Greeley's famous words, "Go West, young man." My childhood included watching Western television classics like *Wagon Trail*, with the great Ward Bond famously yelling, "Wagons ho!" When I was thirty, I did go west, moving to Boise, Idaho, with my family for three years. It was a wonderful experience in so many ways, including driving down the interstate watching the tumbleweeds racing across the landscape. We had the good fortune to visit the Oregon Trail Interpretive Center in Bend, Oregon. The museum was very good, but the highlight was outside the museum, where the ruts from the wagon wheels can still be seen more than one hundred years later. When I started writing this book, I didn't think it would include a story about the Oregon Trail and Decatur County. But I was fortunate to stumble across an 1852 story about locals who left Decatur County, traveling west on the Oregon Trail.

Origen Thomson was one of more than one hundred residents of Decatur County who set out on the adventure of a lifetime in the early spring of 1852. They loved their home, but the call of the Oregon Trail and the incentive of hundreds of free acres of land in Oregon was too tempting to pass up. Origen was just twenty-three years old and unattached, and he was asked by his father to chronicle the journey. Here are a few of my favorite passages from Origen's journal, *Crossing the Plains*.

June 15–17, 1852 Our camp is among the most picturesque scenery that we have yet traveled over, lying on the southwestern side of a vast amphitheatre of hills, a vast concave ten or fifteen miles in diameter, through which, at intervals, can be seen a dark line, formed by the river where it forced its way through the hills, while away to the north the river appears in full view in which place only is the amphitheatre broken. A person would be well paid to leave the trail after passing the spring, turning off to the right and following the river, as he could again strike the trail in fifteen miles. He would see canyons, precipices, falls etc. in fact, nature in all her grandeur is displayed here in the passage of the Platte through the Black Hills.

July 17–19, 1852 There is much beautiful scenery along the trail; the mountain has a varied appearance, reminding one very strongly of a curtain of changeable silk—the red soil appearing through the rich grass I suppose to be the cause of it.

I must admit that my favorite character in *Crossing the Plains* is a man named Sutherland McCoy. You just can't beat someone from Fugit Township who heads west with the courage and adventures of a Kit Carson. If someone was in need, there was Sutherland. If the party needed food, Sutherland was off hunting buffalo or antelope. If a steep ravine needed to be climbed, Sutherland was there. Like many in the party who enjoyed their time in Oregon, Sutherland stayed a handful of years. But as it does for many, home called, and he returned to Indiana. He married a young woman from back home, and they raised their family. This is a description of one of Sutherland's experiences on the Oregon Trail:

At the first crossing, a short time before we came up, a man was hanged by his company. The circumstances are as follows: The murderer had a young man in his employ with whom he had been quarreling all along; yesterday he made it up and became very friendly, and at night asked him to go out into the hills with him. They departed together and the elder came back by himself, after dark, having, as he afterwards confessed, murdered him while the young man was walking before him. In the morning suspicion was aroused, the man acknowledged the act, but boasted that they could not find the body. Search was made, and the body found. Two or three companies coming up a jury was empaneled and the man condemned. They made a gallows by running two or three wagons with their tongues together, so as to make a fork, then locked them so that they could not slip;

the culprit was made to stand on some boxes and the rope put on his neck, and when all was ready the sheriff kicked the boxes from under him and he was launched into eternity. This is the way in which justice is meted out on the Plains—without impediment of legal proceedings.

15

FRED MARLOWE

WORLD WAR I HERO

hen I talk to my students about history, I encourage them to make it personal and learn about their own family history and the contributions they made to their community. I believe that is particularly important as it relates to those who have served in the military in order to preserve our freedoms. Learning about personal history makes it come alive. Understanding history becomes more relevant and real to them. My father was the youngest of seven boys. His father died in a quarry accident when my dad was just six years old. I cannot imagine how challenging that must have been for my grandmother, Alvie Grace Bultman Pratt Narwold. Her children learned respect, the value of hard work and love of country. Dad served in the air force during the Korean War. All six of his brothers served at the same time during World War II, representing the army, navy and marines. Back then, mothers of soldiers who served received a flag with stars on it to reflect the number of their sons serving. The stars were proudly placed in a window of their home. Oh, how I would have loved to have seen that.

My great-great-great-grandfather Jonathon Pratt served during the Revolutionary War and is buried at Prattsburg Cemetery in Ripley County, Indiana. My great-great-uncle Cyrus Baylor was a hero of the War of 1812. My great-uncles Bernard Laudick and Forest Bultman served in World War I. That was supposed to be the war to end all wars. The population of Decatur County at the time was twenty thousand. It still amazes me that Decatur County sent more than one thousand young men to serve. The sacrifices were many, but none as great as the twenty-nine Gold Star families whose young men made the ultimate sacrifice for their country.

The heroism exhibited by our local troops should be honored forever. The following are examples of heroism by those who proudly served during World War I from Decatur County.

Joseph Welsh was the first in the county to be killed in World War I. Our local American Legion post is named in his honor, as well as for Robert Kramer and Wallace Crawley, who went down with the USS *Arizona* on December 7, 1941.

Earl Capper of Letts operated the telegraph that notified the world that the delegates at Versailles had signed the final peace treaty ending World War I. Carl AmRhein received the Medal of Excessive Heroism and Bravery from the French government. In the trenches at Soissons, he was able to successfully break up the enemy's lines. While doing so, he was shot through both thighs and the thumb of his right hand. Walter Moore was wounded by a machine-gun bullet and still managed to single-handedly capture thirty-five Germans.

Then there was Fred Marlowe. The Sandusky Blackhawk graduate was a gunnery sergeant in the Sixth Regular U.S. Marines. On April 1, 1918, he was gassed near Verdun and spent time recovering in five separate French hospitals. He eventually recovered enough to return to his unit and, on November 1, 1918, just days before the end of the war, was with his regiment in a trench near the small French town of Saint Georgies. The Americans had turned the tide in the war since their entry in April 1917, and as 1918 was drawing to a close, the Germans were becoming desperate. It was dawn, and a German machine gun took a shot at Fred. He quickly tore after the soldier firing the machine gun, running through a hedge and into a German trench. He spotted one soldier forty yards away, took careful aim and fired. The bullet hit the soldier's helmet, lifting it in the air some fifteen feet. This wounded the soldier, who began running through the trenches. Sergeant Marlow gave chase and caught up with him as he turned a corner. Marlowe, with his bayonet in place, ordered the German soldier to raise his hands. Seeing other enemy soldiers as well, he grabbed a grenade, held it high and ordered them all to surrender—and they did. It was only then that he realized he had single-handedly captured eighty-four Germans and nine machine guns. As his commander had been wounded, Fred took control. In a letter describing the event to his mother, he wrote, "I didn't get scared until that night about 8 but I did sweat some." For this act of bravery, Fred Marion Marlowe, serving with the American Second Division fighting

Fred Marlowe. *Author collection.*

in the Argonne offensive, received the Distinguished Service Cross for extraordinary heroism. This is our nation's second-highest military award. The war ended on November 11, 1918.

The following year, Fred was still in the service of his country when he was killed in a dynamite accident in Arizona. It was said that the entire county stood still as he was laid to rest in Spring Hill Cemetery. The cemetery is about the halfway point between Sandusky and Clarksburg. He is buried near the road on the northwest side. I encourage you to stop and pay your respects to one of the county's bravest citizens.

16

THE TAYLOR HOTEL

*G*rowing up, my dad, Rex Pratt, always worked a second job. His full-time careers were in finance and real estate. The job I remembered most was his part-time job owning and running the Taylor Hotel in downtown Greensburg. The hotel stood on the southeastern corner of the square and had a storied past. At the original sale of land parcels in 1822, the lot that brought the highest price would eventually be the location of the Taylor Hotel. In fact, it was purchased by the founder of Greensburg himself, Thomas Hendricks. He would later sell the property, and it became a hotel, the Moss House. It was later sold again and became the famous DeArmond Hotel. The hotel was then sold to Mr. Taylor, who renamed it. My dad managed it in the 1960s before eventually owning it. This was the hotel I remember. By then, it largely functioned as a retirement home for low-income older folks. In the 1960s and '70s, there were hardly any agencies set up to help those down on their luck or passing through town without much money. On many nights, I remember Dad receiving calls from local ministers asking for a free night's stay for someone in need. Dad was always happy to oblige.

Even after fifty years, I have so many wonderful memories of the Taylor Hotel. First and foremost were the people. They were all incredibly patient and kind to this little kid hanging around his dad's hotel and were the type who would give the shirt off their back to someone who needed it more than they did. Mary Lou worked the front desk during the day. She had the kind of laugh that filled a room and could cheer a person up even on

From left to right: Helen Keller, Anne Sullivan and Alexander Graham Bell. *Public domain.*

their darkest day. Mr. Hill worked the night shift. The cigar he always had clenched in his mouth made him hard to understand, but he had a great smile. Clyde was the quintessential handyman. I have never seen anyone match his skills. Junior was a great favorite of mine, as he always treated me like a young adult.

The hotel had four floors, with several retail stores on the first floor. Getting my haircut at the barbershop by Bill Strassberger or Don Eubanks was always a treat, especially when they left enough hair to mimic sideburns like my idol, Abraham Lincoln. State Farm Insurance had Dad's friends Tom Simmermeyer and Jerry Abplanalp. Merle Norman Cosmetics had the corner space for decades. Dad's finance office always had the world's nicest ladies working there, like Carol Anne and Delores. In 1980, I ran the local campaign for John Anderson's presidential run, and Dad even gave me an office. "He can't vote, but he can campaign," as the *Greensburg Daily News* described my attempt to help the independent candidate.

A neon hotel sign marked the main entrance. To the right was the phone booth, which looked like it had been installed by Alexander Graham Bell himself. The lobby had about seven lumpy green upholstered chairs, which guaranteed lively conversation day or night. A glass case held candy for sale, and to the right of that was the wooden mailbox. To the left of the lobby were the TV room and the elevator. Riders of the antique elevator had to close the gate to operate it. Walking up the stairs, one reached the second floor, which held another glass case that at one time would have sold toiletries and other essentials. The same bottle of Phillip's Milk of Magnesia sat there for years. The next three floors were the guest rooms. When Dad changed the sheets on the beds, it was my job to dust the spindles on the staircase. Once, in sixth grade, my friend Steve Hellmich and I spent the night in room 318. I remember the room number, because Dad always called room 318 the "premier suite," and I loved it. It had a great corner view of the square. I can envision watching Bobby Kennedy's speech from there. Then I think of the historical icons who stayed there, from President Benjamin Harrison and Vice President Schulyer Colfax to Helen Keller and William Jennings Bryan. Over the bed hung a picture from the 1950s showing an airplane flying by the Statue of Liberty. Dad always loved telling about when Roy Rogers and Dale Evans stayed there—with a bit of embellishment at the end. He'd say, "Roy and Dale stayed in the premier suite of 318, and Trigger stayed across the hall in 301." I don't think I've ever visited the third floor of a hotel without looking for room 318 and thinking of my dad.

17

MEMORIES OF

ROBERT KENNEDY'S VISIT

On May 3, 1968, a great event in the history of Greensburg occurred: a visit and speech from Senator Robert Kennedy. This was the last major presidential candidate to visit the Tree City, but Kennedy was more than a candidate. He represented a vision of a better America, one of peace and respect, one of working together to build a better future for generations to come. Sadly, he was assassinated on June 4, 1968. I asked community members to share their memories of that day. This is what they said.

CHUCK HOOD

We were let out of school to go see him, it was announced on WTRE that morning before school. You could go if you had a ride from a parent. I bummed a ride with a guy's mom. It was quite a festive occasion, with a local band playing. I saw a white pickup truck parked on the south side of the square. I thought, "That's where he will be." So I went and stood by it and didn't leave. Sure enough, when he appeared about forty minutes later, he got up in the bed of the pickup and gave a short speech. He shook my hand twice. I don't recall what he talked about. I guess I was too caught up in the moment. I was in seventh grade that spring of 1968.

ARLEEN SCHWERING

I wish I had a picture, but the moment stays in my mind. My uncle had me on his shoulders during the motorcade visit, and I reached out, and he shook my hand. I was five.

MELODY JOHNSON

I remember it well, because my friend Debbie Cain and I were standing next to the trailer that Senator Kennedy walked up on. Debbie had her hands on the edge of the trailer, and as he walked up on it, he stepped on her fingers.

PAM GOODIN

Mom took us out of school that day to go see Bobby Kennedy, because it was history that probably wouldn't be repeated. He was very gracious and allowed Mom to take a picture of my sister and brother standing next to him. Mom got mad at me, because I refused to stand next to him. I kept looking at all the buildings around the square, feeling as if he would be assassinated, and I refused to stand next to him. Little did I know he would be assassinated a little over a month later. I've often thought about my fears that day and wondered if it was a premonition instead of actual fear.

PHYLLIS HELLMICH

I was privileged to be invited with a group of women to meet Bobby Kennedy at Storie's after he arrived. I have never shook such soft hands. Mr. Kennedy was very kind and gentle to Lucy Shutters when she talked to him about her son Pat they lost in the war.

ANGELA HERSLEY

My dad, Jim Ryle, was privileged to drive Mr. Kennedy around in my grandfather Russell Ryle's light blue convertible. My sisters and brothers and I were still in grade school, but I remember the excitement. A few

Robert Kennedy visit re-creation. *Author collection.*

This is another view of the Robert Kennedy visit re-creation. *Author collection.*

Robert Kennedy campaigns in Greensburg. *Courtesy of the* Greensburg Daily News.

gentlemen from Robert's campaign committee came to our house the night before to check out the car in the garage. My sister, Nancy Ryle Tower, was home at the time of his arrival because of an appendectomy, so she got to go to the airport here to greet him. The rest of us went downtown, and I just remember older kids in the trees on the square. It was a memory that we will never forget.

CHRISTY DUNNE

I was six years old and so excited….I thought he was so handsome and I must have thought he was a prince. My parents took us to the square and I got to touch his hand. I will never forget his face.

18

FAVORITE MOVIE MEMORIES

*O*ne of the true joys of growing up in the twentieth century was a visit to the movie theater. The smell of the popcorn, hearing the clicking of the film reel, enjoying the taste of Milk Duds or a soda pop from the fountain—and that was before the movie even began. There is something truly magical about the entire movie experience. I, like all of you, experience a flood of memories rushing to my mind when I think of those early movie memories in Greensburg. Growing up in the late 1960s/early 1970s meant that I was able to experience the Tree Theater.

Going to the movies was a treat, so I remember most every one I saw as a kid. John Wayne never looked as good as he did on the big screen in *True Grit*. I owe my love of horror movies to my older brothers, Tom and Mike, who took me to see Christopher Lee and Veronica Carlson in *Dracula Has Risen from the Grave*. I would love to get an orange soda with crushed ice from that fountain drink machine just one more time.

My mom and dad, Rex and Lucille, met at the Tree. Dad and a friend sat behind Mom and her friend and threw popcorn at them. The name of the movie was *The Bridge on the River Kwai*. So, by the end of the show, Rex and Lucille had made a love connection, and as they say, the rest is history. They were married for over forty years and had five children and eleven grandchildren. I'd say that story turned out pretty well

Sadly, by the time I went to Greensburg Junior High, the Tree had closed. There would be movie memories in high school, but those would mean traveling to Batesville, Shelbyville or Indianapolis to see a show. I belong to a Facebook group called "Greensburg Memories." Members shared some of their favorite Greensburg Theater moments. Here are a few of my favorites.

HELEN BLACK

I remember the cool balcony seats at the K of P Theater. Also one time, the entire St. Mary's School walked the two blocks to the Tree Theater to see *Lily of the Fields* with Sydney Poitier.

LOGAN HYATT

The Tree Theater used to have a night one day a week when they would draw ticket numbers for $100. My father and I went to every one of these nights and never did win, but I saw every bad and good movie of the early mid-'60's (*Beach Blanket Bingo*, etc.).

Also, Greensburg was not known for having lots to do in those days. (Sitting in the car on the square watching people was a biggie.) However both the movie house and the funeral homes had an outdoor marquee. We would drive by the theater and see what was showing there and drive by the funeral home and see who was showing there. I went to so many wakes/funerals of people I didn't know.

BARB JONES

I always remember the story my dad (Lewis Clark)—or better known as Fuzzy, was born and raised in Greensburg—was at the Tree Theater on December 7th when Pearl Harbor was bombed, and they announced it and he lived on South Broadway and he walked home and talked to his mother (Grace) about joining the army to fight for his country. I cherish all the many stories he told.

MARK HAMER

Mom and Dad owned Family Affair Ceramic Studio. Their storefront was right next to the fire department, which at that time was on that first block of South Broadway. My dad would often spend parts of his weekend there at the studio, pouring, firing, etc. I'd sometimes whine about there being nothing to do and being bored. Or perhaps overstayed my welcome at the Greensburg Fire Department—they had an attraction there called a fireman's pole. Dad would sometimes send me across the alley to the Tree Theater. Even after all these years I can still remember the smell (not malodorous) there, the popcorn was made not far from the front door. The soft drink vending machine and the pellet ice it dispensed. This is also where I learned of the Motion Picture Association and movie ratings and how evidently some movies would warp my mind?

DARYL MARTIN

One Saturday morning, my folks dropped me off at the Tree to see *Journey to the Center of the Earth*. Before the movie, the theater had a drawing for prizes. I won a croquet set with a wheeled carrier. During the movie, one of the croquet balls got loose and rolled down to the front of the theater. Later, it made walking home to First Street rather challenging. Kept the croquet set a long time.

KIM GROSS SCHAFFER

My first time at the movies was there with my grandma to watch *Mary Poppins*. I saw *The Wizard of Oz* there, and I swear I sucked all the air from the room when she landed in Oz and it was in color. Our TV was black and white.

GINGER STEWART WEBB

My grandmother Dora Wilson fixed a huge Sunday dinner every week. She had a very large family and expected everyone who lived close to be there. After an amazing meal, the younger cousins went to Tree Theater for the matinee. The matinee was at a discounted price, so this made it affordable. We had an amazing time, and it gave the adults time to visit uninterrupted.

After the movies we would walk up to Murphy's department store, where I would purchase a bracelet for five cents or an Evening in Paris perfume for ten cents (the remainder of my movie money.) These are some of my fondest memories.

Bob Siefker

During the summer of 1960, the Tuxis youth group of First Presby was blessed with two fabulous advisors, John and Pat Smyser (you know her today as Pat Smith). In truth, they weren't that much older than we were! Our pastor, Don Newhouse, was another young man and was open to things that we came up with.

During a brainstorming meeting the previous winter, someone suggested making a movie. Fred Craig, then one of the youth, had the know-how and equipment, and with Pat and John's help, a script was written, location sheets made, casting calls, wardrobe, et cetera.

Tower Tree no. 2. *Courtesy of Daniel Fayette.*

By summertime, we were ready to start shooting!

Once all the scenes were "in the can," Fred edited the movie and Don Newhouse narrated it. Mike Ewing, Fred, Don and I spent a day or two in the high school library adding the soundtrack.

In the movie, the two star-crossed lovers meet at the Tree Theater watching a movie titled *The Atomic Spider*!

19

FAVORITE RESTAURANT MEMORIES

*T*he Tree City in the late 1960s and early 1970s was a wonderful, safe, blue-collar community. My mother had her hands full raising five children, and she was a great cook. Still, it was a huge treat to go out to eat. I remember each New Year's Day: a full day of football games to watch also meant a bucket of the Colonel's fried chicken with all the trimmings. At the time I attended Greensburg High School we had open lunch, meaning we could go out to eat. Hardly a Monday went by that we did not get the taco and burrito special at Pizza King. I still remember the wonderful combination with a Big Red drink. Sometimes, we ventured next door to Burger Chef. No matter where we ate, we enjoyed getting away from school and having a great meal with friends.

When the Pratt family moved back to Greensburg in 1999, a new food tradition was born. My wife, Jill, became the children's librarian at the Greensburg Public Library, a job she absolutely loves. But that also meant working Monday evenings providing story time. That meant Dad was in charge of dinner. I'm no cook, so on Mondays, Clare, Caroline and I would be faced with that difficult decision: where to get dinner. Sometimes we had fast food, but the local restaurants conjure up the best memories. Dairy Point, Story's, Pizza King and Great Wall were favorites. There is something special about memories from restaurants in a community, so I asked people to share some of theirs. Here are some of my favorites.

EDITH RUTHERFORD

My best memory is when I went with my dad to Kentucky Fried Chicken and we sat there and talked. It's been torn down, but the memories are still with me.

MICHAEL CORNN

Back in the day (won't say how long ago), after every home Pirate basketball game, the family would go to Pasquale's Pizza.

FANNY McDANIEL

Keilors!!! I never switched to calling it Storie's....The only hard thing about going to Keilors was trying to decide whether to have a piece of coconut cream pie or a chocolate sundae. Another memory about Keilors was the mirror out front. If you stood ½ bodies in front of it and lifted your leg and arm, it looked like you were jumping up and down with both legs off the ground....Don't laugh, you know you did it!

PATRICK NOBBE

A&W Drive-In. There are more than a few marriages that originated from this establishment, my family being one of them.

TAYLOR HAUCK

Every payday Friday when my dad got off at 3:00 from James River/Printpack, he would pick us up from the babysitters and take us for ice cream at Doodlebuddies. I was in grade school, not sure when the shop closed. I always got cookies and cream, and my sister got superman!

Greensburg, Indiana courthouse. *Courtesy of Daniel Fayette.*

DEBORAH KELLAR

In the '70s, I worked as a carhop at a restaurant/hangout called Leo's Ranch on Lincoln Street. It was owned by Bertha and Jim Wilhoit. On the weekends, "teenagers" drove up and down Lincoln and used Leo's Ranch as a turnaround to continue their cruising the strip.

LAURA FOSTER

Pizza King! There were always a few restaurants that you missed when you went away for college. Pizza King was one of them. I could not wait to have their tacos or burritos. They are not the same anywhere else. Pizza King was the place to go to after home games to hang out with friends. Pizza King was where I remember crowding into a car next to my future husband to go take a lap on the strip. Pizza King was the place my future husband and I had our first date and my bridal shower.

MICHELLE SCHUTTE-CATHEY

For me it was 1980 something, and it was Dairy Point. My grandma Dugle lived across the street, and she would always send us over with money to get whatever we wanted. At the time they had a huge candy counter. I remember buying baseball and Garbage Pail Kids cards and of course a twist cone. No place to this day has better ice cream sprinkles than them.

20

DID YOU KNOW?

*I*always thought I knew quite a bit about our local history. But in writing this book, I am amazed at the kernels of information that I have found. This book is not meant to be a comprehensive history but rather my favorite stories from the perspective of a high school history teacher who finds great value in relating local history to my students. There certainly is not room for all of the interesting stories and tidbits, so I added this section of quick, fun facts about Decatur County that I found especially interesting. I hope you do, too.

- In 1835, the first known antislavery society in Indiana was organized in Kingston.
- The town of Burney can proudly claim All-American Girl Professional Baseball League All-Star Janet Rumsey and President Eisenhower's surgeon general, LeRoy Burney, as proud former residents. Burney's Chautauqua once hosted composer and bandleader John Philip Sousa.
- B.B. Harris, a scout for Morgan's Raiders who entered Decatur County, came back after the war to establish Harris City and the Harris City Stone Quarry. His former home on Franklin Street in Greensburg is in the National Register of Historic Places.
- Greensburg claimed to host the first community spelling match in the country. A famous event occurred in 1875 in the courthouse, when Susie F. Wise of New Penington won the

B.B. Harris Home. *Courtesy of Daniel Fayette.*

match over lawyers, doctors, teachers and others and won 160 acres of western land owned by James Hart.

- Madge Rutherford Minton of Greensburg, member of the World War II WASPs, was one of the first four women in the United States to graduate from the Advanced Civilian Pilot Training Program.

- On June 23, 1919, Earl Capper, Company A, 113th Field Signal Battalion, 38th Division, stationed in LeHavre, France, received the message of the signing of the Treaty of Versailles. He relayed it to the world by telegraph.

- Surgeon General Dr. LeRoy Burney, a Burney High School graduate, announced that there is a link between tobacco and cancer. He was the first to do so, on July 15, 1957.

- Wendell Osborn of Greensburg graduated from the United States Naval Academy in 1927, where he was a three-year football letterman. He rose to be lieutenant commander of the USS *Juneau*. It was sunk on November 13, 1942, during the Battle of Guadalcanal. He was one of the 687 men killed along with the 5 Sullivan brothers.

Right: Madge Rutherford Minton. *Courtesy of Find a Grave*.

Below: The courthouse in Greensburg. *Will Lemay (photo released into public domain)*.

- Mary Stewart Carey, who was born in Greensburg in 1859 (her family moved to Indianapolis when she was three), was the founder of the world-renowned Indianapolis Children's Museum.
- Terri Kanouse, a 1978 North Decatur graduate, was the University of Nebraska's first All-American volleyball player.
- David Letterman's first broadcasting job was at WTRE Radio.
- Rose McConnell Long, the third woman to serve in the United States Senate, was from Greensburg.
- The first tree seen on the Courthouse Tower was in 1870. The tower has never been without a tree since.
- Decatur County is home to Larry Sparks, member of the Bluegrass Hall of Fame.
- Mrs. Justus Rich was probably the first doctor in the county, practicing medicine in Greensburg as early as 1821 or 1822.
- By 1850, Jane Speed, an African American living in Fugit Township, had become one of the largest landowners, with eighty acres. She was also a pillar of the Underground Railroad.
- David Robert Lewis, 1879 Greensburg High School graduate, was the first African American graduate of Purdue University. He received a BS in civil engineering.

21

HOOSIER HYSTERIA

MY FAVORITE PIRATE TEAM

I had the honor of being a teacher at Greensburg High School when the basketball team won back-to-back 3A State Championships in 2013 and 2014. I had the pleasure of teaching most of the players, and all were excellent students and fine young men. The excitement of their runs created some Hoosier hysteria right here in Greensburg, just like in the games of old. Class basketball came to Indiana at the close of the 1997 season. Trust me, there are many positives with class ball. More trophies mean more athletes can experience the joy of cutting down the nets. Still, it's not like it was when the whole country looked at Indiana as the pinnacle of high school basketball.

In the late 1960s and '70s, I would go with my dad to the games. Each game was an event—great players, a large student section and the town virtually shut down because everyone was at the gym. Making those days even more special was the high level of competition. From 1937 to 1977, Greensburg belonged to the powerhouse South Central Conference. Conference teams included state champions prior to class: Bloomington, Bloomington North, Connersville, Franklin, Martinsville, Shelbyville, Jeffersonville and Indianapolis Washington. Greencastle, Southport, Seymour, Columbus and 1976 state final runner-up Rushville were the other members with Greensburg. It is mind-boggling to realize that these historic programs gave us John Wooden, Chuck Taylor, the Wonder Five and Bill Garrett. At times, this could have arguably been considered the best conference in the state. That made Greensburg's conference titles few and far between, but one year, the Pirates were the sole champions. That year was 1949. The conference championship was and still is determined by the best record in each individual conference.

I grew up in awe of this team, as I knew their leading scorer, my dad, Rex Pratt. I always loved hearing Dad's stories of sinking shots from the coffin corner, as it was called. After his freshman year, Dad's family moved to Napoleon. He helped lead the Napoleon Bearcats to back-to-back Ripley County championships. After his junior year, the Pirates came calling, and he answered, playing his senior year for Greensburg.

The 1948–49 Pirates set team records in average points and total points scored. The schedule had to have been one of the toughest in the state. Besides conference teams, they also played two programs that won state championships, Madison, and New Castle, as well as teams like East Chicago Roosevelt, Batesville, Lawrenceburg and 1947 runner-up Terre Haute Garfield. Big wins that year included Franklin, Seymour, Columbus and Terre Haute Garfield. I always wished that the school could have held a reunion of the team so that I could have heard the stories from all of the forty-niners: Jerry Westhafer, John Moeller, Bob Ricke, Carl Overpeck,

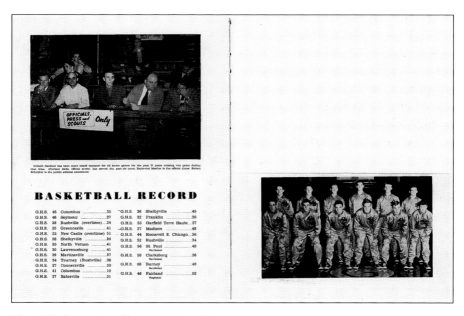

The 1949 Greensburg Pirates. *Author collection.*

Frank Manus, Earl Borden, Jack Williams, Gene Best, Bob Platt, Dale Mount and Coach Tom Downey.

I like how the sectional comprised all the Decatur County schools. Greensburg was much bigger than the other schools, so it won the majority of the titles. But every so often, Sandusky, Clarksburg or another small school would win. Those had to be cherished memories. In the 1949 Greensburg Sectional, the Pirates got wins over St. Paul, Clarksburg and Burney. The regional result was not what was hoped for, as they fell to Fairland, 52–46. Fairland had just one regular-season loss. John Moeller was always Dad's best friend, and he became the first Pirate to be named to the Indiana All-Star Team. John Moeller and Rex Pratt were named All-Conference, All-Sectional and All-Regional.

Every day for my four years attending Greensburg High School, I entered the north doors and walked by the trophy case where the '49 South Central Conference Championship trophy sat in a place of high honor. After Dad died in 1999, we were able to borrow the trophy for the visitation. The trophy depicted a classic player in vintage clothes. Sadly, the trophy went missing about ten years ago. I sure would love to go back in time to that 1948–'49 season and see Dad hit one from coffin corner.

Part II

GROWING UP IN GREENSBURG

22

BASEBALL AND BICYCLES

At 10:00 p.m. on warm summer nights, the last light would go dark at North Park in Greensburg. Each summer for many years, these three baseball diamonds were my second home. Who needed a movie theater or even cable television when there was always a baseball game to be played or watched? I have so many wonderful memories playing for the Sox, Stars, Colts and Dodgers. One of my best memories is of my favorite uncle seeing me short-hop the fence. I knew how Tinkers, Evers and Chance felt when the infield included Barry Blackburn, Tom and Tony O'Mara and me. My greatest game was in Little League as a pitcher for the Sox. I was never the fastest pitcher but was proud of my windup. Just like Juan Marichal, I would kick my front foot high in the air with precision and aim for the strike zone. One hot summer night, I faced the Astros. Their star was the home run king, Clint Tichenor. His muscles were about four times the size of mine, and his swing was as sweet as the Great Bambino's. The first four times I faced Clint that day, he hit solo home runs off me. He really had my number. Still, I was undaunted and rolled through the rest of the lineup. It was the bottom of the ninth, I was still pitching and we had the lead, 6–4. They were knocking me around pretty good by then. With one out and the bases loaded, Shorty Jackson came to the plate. He had been to the plate fifty times that season and had walked every single at-bat. He did this by bending down and making himself as low as possible, leaving about a three-inch strike zone. The count was full, I kicked high and I heard the umpire yell, "Strike three!" It was a joyous moment that quickly faded as the

North Park. *Courtesy of Daniel Fayette.*

next batter, my nemesis, Clint Tichenor, came up. Two outs, bottom of the ninth, bases loaded, a 6–4 lead. Clint had already hit four long balls against me. Then Coach Heaton gave the sign—we would intentionally walk him, making the score 6–5. The crowd seemed stunned. Who walks a batter with the bases loaded? Only Coach Heaton did, because he knew who was on the mound. The batter after Tichenor quickly hit a lazy fly ball to centerfield that was caught by the coach's son Brian. Victory was ours! Those victories were always a little sweeter, literally, as winners received free large Pepsis from the concession stand. The losers got small Pepsis. But I digress. It is 10:00 p.m., and the last light has been turned off.

The bike ride home by the neighborhood gang rivaled the action at North Park that night. In those days, we didn't lock our doors and the children were safe at night. I owned three bikes in my life. The first I bought for five dollars at a garage sale. I don't know what brand it was, because the twenty-inch frame had been spray-painted royal blue. That bike was made for speed and made for me. To most people, the fact that it didn't have working brakes would have been a concern, but in the 1970s, that only added to the adventure of riding it. It was imperative that I had a good pair of sneakers in case I needed to stop quickly. The route from Carver Street to the 500 block of East Washington Street is about a mile and a half. With sufficient twists and turns, it had the feel of a European road race. There was no need to play a video game if one could live it, although I must admit I always did enjoy a thrilling game of Pong. Of course, the highlight of the ride home was reaching maximum speed down North Street's hill, followed by crossing the busiest street in town, Lincoln. I sure am glad my mother never saw me doing that on a bike with no brakes. I did eventually buy a bigger bike for ten dollars. It was a beautiful shade of orange and had brakes. It just lacked handlebars. Looking back, it's hard to choose which I liked best.

23

A FOOTBALL STORY

I grew up in a sports-minded family, so in the late 1960s and early '70s, there was no shortage of outdoor games and sports of all kinds. My father, Rex, was a great basketball player who played some ball at Franklin College and Indiana State University. My two older brothers, Mike and Tom, were better than me in most sports, as was younger brother Jim. Sister Susan was a good tennis player. Tennis was the only sport in which I excelled, thanks in large part to my high school coach, George Granholt. So why in the world have I chosen to write about my one year in organized football? It all comes down to one memorable game. But first, some backstory.

In Greensburg in the 1970s, the organized youth football league was flag football. My dad probably never said this, but I think it was implied: "Pratts don't play flag football." So I never played in that league. Growing up, there were plenty of pickup games, all tackle. I graduated from St. Mary's Elementary School after completing the sixth grade. In seventh grade, the kids from the public elementary schools and St. Mary's attended Greensburg Junior High School together. A few weeks before school started, the newspaper ran an article about tryouts for the seventh-grade football team. The possibility of playing on the team became a topic of conversation in our household. I believe my part of the conversation included me saying that I did not want to play, but it was decided that it would be "good" for me. So, on a hot summer afternoon in 1975, I went to my first practice.

There's a great scene in the movie *Rudy*, when the groundskeeper has a heart-to-heart moment with Rudy and says, "You're five foot nothin', 100 and nothin',," meaning he was short and skinny. Well, that was me. Even with pads and a helmet, I couldn't have intimidated the grasshoppers on the practice field. When everyone marched onto the field, it looked to me like there were one hundred guys trying out. Our head coach was Bill Edwards. He was a fantastic seventh-grade social studies teacher and junior high coach. Mr. Edwards split the boys into two groups, one for quarterbacks, receivers and running backs, and one for the offensive line. I must have been nervous, so I paused and somehow ended up with the big guys in the offensive line group.

The offensive and defensive line coach was Mr. Hoffman, whom I regard to this day as one of the nicest people I have ever known. But I was not used to the tough football drills he had in store for us. I never had any hair on my chest, and I knew I never would, because I survived those practices without growing any. The football season was short, just six games. My role was to be a reserve offensive guard and inside lineman. Our star at those positions was Geoff Mouser, so when the season began, I knew I would be enjoying the view from the sidelines.

As was usual with a Mr. Edwards team, we dominated the early games and raced to a 5-0 start. I had yet to play, but I was fine with that. Game six was against the other powerhouse in the league, the Connersville Spartans. It was a home game, the last of the season. The game was a physical, back-and-forth confrontation. But then something changed. "Pratt, you're in!" called out Mr. Edwards. I couldn't believe it, but it was true, I was going in! Geoff Mouser had been injured. Shock, fear and horror were my feelings at that moment, but go in I did. My job now was inside linebacker. As such, I was to break through the block of the guard and tackle the running back.

The perspective on the field was very different at night than during our daytime practices. Still, I could see well enough to notice that the other team had something we did not: facial hair, especially the one right across the line from me. I'm still not convinced he was a seventh-grader. Did I take some hits that night? Sure I did. But just like Rudy, I kept getting back up. Tackling their two-hundred-pound halfback was both challenging and rewarding. When the final gun went off, the Pirates ended the season with a perfect 6-0 record. Perhaps even more miraculously, I was still standing. You may wonder if I continued in my football career. Thankfully, I retired at the age of thirteen, destined for pickup football games in the neighborhood and eventually the tennis court, where tackling your opponent is frowned upon.

24

MY PET, KILLER

*I*n my household, we love traditions, especially at Christmas. One of these is watching the movie *A Christmas Story*. Based on a book written by the great Hoosier author Jean Shepherd, it follows the main character, Ralphie, and his quest to find a Red Ryder BB gun under the Christmas tree. I think all of us have treasured memories of that one gift that will always be remembered. For me, it was Killer.

My uncle Herold and aunt Jeanette never had any children of their own, so on Christmas morning, our family of seven became a family of nine. They spent every Christmas with us. Uncle Harold was the only one who called me Johnny Bill (my name is John William). Basketball was the official sport of the Pratt family, and Uncle Harold would give us a dollar for every ten points we scored in a game. My two older brothers cleaned up over the years. As for me, I took in a grand total of one dollar in my five years of playing organized basketball. Still, as I look back, it was I who received the greatest Christmas gift of all from Uncle Harold and Aunt Jeanette. At the age of seven, I was given a live alligator.

Naming the reptile was the easy part. I knew this gator had a heart of gold but jaws that could kill. So, Killer seemed like the perfect name for him. He was about eighteen inches long and loved to be in the water. The only problem with this was that he took over the bathtub. I loved Killer, but after about ten days with a family of seven not bathing, it soon became apparent that Killer could not stay. Uncle Harold and Aunt Jeanette had purchased him in Florida and said they would be happy to take him back there. Once a year after that for several years, Uncle Harold and Aunt Jeanette would come over and set up their eight-millimeter projector and screen, and we would watch a home movie of an alligator farm. Uncle Harold would yell out, "That one is Killer!" My alligator always looked happy and well cared for. I was much older when I learned the truth: Killer had been set free in Greensburg's Gas Creek. So, if you hear a rural legend about an alligator sunning itself on the banks of Gas Creek, you know its Killer! If you do see him, tell him John says "hey."

25

TENNIS BALL

Growing up in the late 1960s and '70s in Greensburg was really the end of the era of not worrying about locking doors and worrying about children playing outside until dark. By high school, most of our athletic contests were associated with school on organized teams. Still, the boys in my neighborhood could always play a game of what will always be affectionately known as "Tennis Ball."

During the summer before fourth grade, we moved to East Washington Street. Neighbors helped neighbors, and just two doors down from our house was Baldwin's empty lot. Billie Baldwin was just about the nicest person you could ever hope to meet. She owned the lot, and her house was next to it. To me, the empty lot was more important than the house, although Mrs. Baldwin might have felt differently. But perhaps not. At any time, she could have sold the lot for the construction of a new house, but she loved to hear the sound of children playing. All kinds of sports were played there, but it was the game of Tennis Ball that I most fondly recall. The game is just baseball played with a tennis ball with a few tweaks added. All players must bat left-handed, and it is slow-pitch. The vast majority of us were right-handed, so the occasional lefty who played had a distinct advantage. This also kept most of the balls to right and center fields. Left field was short, and a well-hit ball could rattle the neighbor's house. Maybe that is why they accumulated a huge collection of tennis balls, as any ball that hit the top of their hill would rarely be seen again. Left field dropped off to a ten-foot hill behind second base, making for phenomenal "game of the week" catches.

A maple tree between right and left fields needed to be avoided, or else the outfielder would end up in the emergency room. But the best fielders heard the ball through the leaves and caught it on the way out. Just to the right of the tree was the coveted Wickens fence. A ball hit there was an automatic home run. It comprised a bit less than half of right field, so only the most seasoned sluggers could trot around the bases.

Tennis Ball players were as loyal to the game as Brooklyn Dodger fans. We were masters of our chosen sport. Carl, Paul, Lou, Jim, Gary, Sammy, Mark, Craig, Brian, Trevor and so many others made up our select group. Carl would bring an old glove for me to use. The mitt read, "Darryl Rice is nice." Pitcher was my primary position, probably because of my intimidating Juan Marichal–esque delivery. We played rain or shine, and I remember pitching once in a steady drizzle. The wet grass made for awesome diving catches that day. In fact, I made the dive of my career that day, but a jagged piece of glass ripped open my leg, requiring fifty stitches. Yes, I did catch the ball. And yes, they finished the game without me.

Once, I was pitching on a beautiful summer day when a not-so-friendly bumble bee began flying around my head. This bee was in attack mode, and I could not shake it. I took off in a full sprint to my house, rushed inside and slammed the door. After a brief sigh of relief, I heard something next to my ear: "bzzzzz." The bee had followed me into the house! I swatted it through the entry room, the TV room, then into the kitchen. At this point, I knew it was him or me. I drew on an inner strength, caught the bee between two fingers and killed it. Tennis Ball created a lifetime of memories.

The pinnacle of Tennis Ball history was our first World Series. I was captain of the Cubs, and Paul was the captain of the Reds. A successful draft ensured a series that would be remembered for years to come. Billie Baldwin threw out the first pitch, a moment caught by a beautiful action photo seen in the *Greensburg Daily News*. Paul blasted the National Anthem, courtesy of Jimi Hendrix. We stood at attention in our specially made shirts, cherishing the moment—one of the last before adulthood came and we went our separate ways. I cannot remember who won the series, but I can assure you that it was well played, with home runs and diving catches. A few years later, Mrs. Baldwin died and the lot was sold. A house was built and trees planted. I remember those days of no officials, no parents, no scorebooks, no trophies, no travel teams, just the fun of a game of Tennis Ball. Those were the good old days.

26

ST. MARY'S SCHOOL ADVENTURES

I loved my one year of public school kindergarten at Rosenmund Elementary School. I loved my teacher, Mrs. Smith, even though I never got my shoe icon on the blackboard for learning to tie my shoe, but I was always good at finger painting. Mike Knecht and I went to the first day together and found kindergarten to be an amazing place, unlike every other student in the class, all of whom were crying. My goal that year was perfect attendance. I mean, who wouldn't want to go to kindergarten every day? I went to school in the afternoon. One day, I woke up with a temperature of 103 degrees. But I was bound and determined to be well by noon. With the help of my mom, I was. I will never forget the last day of school. Mrs. Smith presented me with the award for perfect attendance. With my mother watching proudly, I accepted a huge, beautiful ABC book. Now that was a good day. But this chapter is about St. Mary's, so on to first grade.

Riding a school bus with your two older brothers meant you had made it to the big leagues. We were the last to be picked up in the morning by good old "Dutch," the driver of bus no. 9. From first through sixth grade, I attended St. Mary's School. Catholic schools in the early 1970s still had plenty of nuns, from the sweet Sister Francesca to the disciplinarian Sister Agnissa. As we Hoosiers say about Abe Lincoln's time in Indiana, these were my formative years.

In first and second grades, recess was in the small area by the convent. It was a memorable day when three hundred children lined up to see a moon landing on the one television in the convent. Third grade was time to graduate to the big playground and to master the art of kickball. I had the distinction of being in the elite club of kickers who broke a window in the school. I had to go to the rectory and tell Father Geis, shaking all the way. To his credit and my relief, he wasn't angry.

St. Mary's had an unofficial theme song. It went something like this: "Run, run, run, I think I see a nun, pick up your bottles and run. If Father should appear say Father have a beer, on the playground at St. Mary's School." I have so many amazing memories of St. Mary's, but the most memorable was the last day of sixth grade. My good friend Steve Hellmich and I decided to commemorate our last day with specially made T-shirts. The 1970s was the beginning of the boom of the T-shirt industry, including in downtown Greensburg. Hoosier Sporting Goods was the place to go. Its walls were filled with classic iron-on decals, from the peace sign to "Keep on Truckin'." But one design stood out above the rest to Steve and me: "U.S. Streaking Team." Ah, that crazy 1970s fad. The craze was forever captured in the classic Ray Stevens song, "The Streak." We bought bright orange T-shirts with "U.S. Streaking Team" on the back. We decided to choose our own wording for the front. In big, bold block letters, the front of my shirt read, "St. Mary's Prison Camp." The words filled most of the front of the shirt. My masterpiece was now complete. The question that

St. Mary's School. *Courtesy of Daniel Fayette.*

remained was, would we be able to successfully wear it for the last day of school. And what were the possible repercussions of this creativity? Could this end up in our "permanent record?" Worse yet, could we be forced to repeat the sixth grade?!

The morning of the last day went smoothly, as the shirts garnered attention but no trouble. The true test would come at lunchtime. I remember exactly where I sat in the cafeteria, second row from the front, twelfth seat from the left, facing all incoming traffic. Right on schedule, Sister Mary Raymond, principal of St. Mary's, walked into the cafeteria. With a reputation as an excellent educator, she could be tough but was also fair. She stopped and stared right at me for what felt like five minutes. She then turned her head and kept walking without saying a word. I will always remember and respect her for allowing us our small act of rebellion.

27

LINCOLN'S BOYHOOD HOME TRIP

I remember the day I first went to the Greensburg Carnegie Public Library. Martha Samuels was the librarian. There were books as far as the eye could see. There must have been thousands of them! The main floor was clearly for adults and very quiet. Downstairs was filled with more colors, and the children's librarian greeted me with a smile. (Greensburg Library's current children's librarian meets me with a smile every day, as we've been married for thirty-three years!) I was quickly attracted to the biographies. I always loved history and reading about inspirational people. Then I saw the book that would change the course of my life: *Abraham Lincoln*. I pored over that book many times, learning as much about the man as I could take in.

I had a wonderful childhood, but as we were five kids and Dad worked two jobs, vacations were scarce. Twice we went to the sites in Kentucky: My Old Kentucky Home, Fort Harrod, Shaker Village and, of course, Abraham Lincoln's birthplace. Each time, we experienced an outdoor amphitheater performance, once *My Old Kentucky Home* and then *Daniel Boone*. I was even lucky enough to get a coonskin cap as a souvenir. Oh, how I loved that hat!

The summer between fifth and sixth grades, Mom and Aunt Carolyn took me and my younger sister and brother, Susan and Jim, to southern Indiana. We started with a stop at Indiana's first state capitol, Corydon. The Civil War conflicts at Corydon and Gettysburg were the only two battles fought on Northern soil. We also visited Spencer County and Santa Claus Land. At that time, the park was much smaller and very quaint. Honestly, it was more my cup of tea than the large theme park that is there today, but I do love unlimited soft drinks.

From there, it was on to the Abraham Lincoln National Boyhood Memorial in Kentucky. Of course, everyone knows that Abe spent his crucial formative years, from ages seven to eighteen, in Indiana. It was in Indiana that he developed his passion for learning. There was a wonderful small replica village at the site. His mother, whom he loved very much, is buried here. It was also here that my mother surprised me with an amazing gift, an Abraham Lincoln gold-plated bust. If I was not hooked for life as a Lincoln fan before, I was now. That night, we had the rare treat of sleeping in a hotel. I remember all of us telling stories, just like Abe would, and Mom laughing so hard she cried. Now that was a good day.

28

THE CYCOS

*M*usical venues through the years have delighted and entertained generations with the performances they provide: Carnegie Hall, the Hollywood Bowl, the Sydney Opera House and, of course, the Pratts' upstairs bathroom. Much like in Liverpool with the Beatles, it was on the playground at St. Mary's School in the fourth grade that Wade Ryle and I decided to form a band, and the CYCOS (pronounced "psychos") were born.

At first, we wrote many of our own songs. We combined them with classics as well as some comedy. Our main venue was our upstairs bathroom. It had a capacity of ten chairs. We would make our grand entrance by coming in from the attic. Our opening song was the same as Elvis's. (I'm not sure, but I think Elvis used it first.) Wade and I could both belt out pretty mean renditions of Elvis classics. I was always partial to the ballads, such as *Love Me Tender*. In the early days, we did comedy routines. I remember Cheech and Chong's "Sister Mary Elephant" well.

We wrote songs mostly about classmates, one of which went, "Once upon a time, there was a man named Wade Ryle. He had a girl and her name was Lisa." "Going to Jail" was another big hit for him. My top hit was "Nickel Machine." I'll never forget the command performance at a junior high dance. It went, "Oh, now I put on my tux and my silver tie. When I go out I tell my parents a lie / I get in the car and I'm passing by / The next thing you know, a girl's saying hi / So I put in a nickel in the nickel machine / And it said 'Love, Love, Love, it's the name of the game.' / It said 'Love, Love' when you put in a nickel in the nickel machine." Those were some great lyrics.

The CYCOS had many managers, and then Kimball joined on the drums. We rocked the Decatur County Democratic Party's summer picnic. Then came our big break, playing the main stage as the halftime entertainment at the Mr. Decatur County Contest. For the big show, we recruited Bruce to play the bass. His brother Tim was on the piano. We knew we were a hit as the crowd roared!

Alas, stardom was not to be. After that, just like John, Paul, George and Ringo, it was time to call it quits. Sometimes, I wonder whatever became of those two eight-track tapes we made.

A 365-DAY CALENDAR OF
IMPORTANT EVENTS IN
DECATUR COUNTY HISTORY

January 1, 1963—Judge John Goddard organizes two new school corporations, Greensburg and Decatur County Community Schools.

January 2, 1963—John William Pratt, third son of Rex and Lucille Pratt, is the first baby born that year at Decatur County Memorial Hospital.

January 3, 1899—The first known use of the word *automobile* appears in an editorial in the *New York Times*. The following year, Ira J. Hollensbe of Greensburg purchased the first commercially made steam-powered automobile in the country. Gasoline-powered cars began production in 1901.

January 4, 1913—Sergeant Lawrence Fry, U.S. Army, of Millhousen, is born. He was killed in action during World War II on September 22, 1944.

January 5, 1935—Arnold Bredewater scores a season-high 21 points as the New Point Little Giants defeat Oldenburg, 72–14.

January 6, 1967—After trailing 61–65 to Columbus, with fifty-two seconds left, the Pirate basketball team comes storming back and wins on a ten-foot fadeaway by Bob Barker, 67–66.

January 7, 1842—Jacob Overturf, Medal of Honor recipient, is born.

January 8, 2021—Beloved former Pirate basketball coach Phil Snodgress is laid to rest.

January 9, 1862—Amos Gregg Conner, Company E, Seventh Indiana Infantry, dies of disease in Grafton, West Virginia.

Ira J. Hollensbe. *Courtesy of Daniel Fayette.*

January, 10 1879—Tony Stewert was the first person pictured with the tree on the courthouse tower, appearing in the local newspaper.

January 11, 1916—Lowell Beard of Westport is born. The U.S. Army Technician Fourth Grade was killed in action on July 25, 1943.

January 12, 1874—Carl Graham Fisher, son of Albert and Ida Fisher, was born in Greensburg, Indiana. He would go on to create the Indianapolis Motor Speedway and the Indianapolis 500.

January 13, 1936—More than one hundred customers start Decatur County REMC.

January 14, 1938—In hoops action, Jackson defeats Letts, 41–15, led by William Howe's 13 points. The team went 22-3 and was led in scoring with Ralph Phillips's 214 points.

January 15, 2003—The television show *Ripley's Believe It or Not!* airs a segment featuring the tree on the courthouse tower.

January 16, 1954—The New Point basketball Giants defeat Clarksburg, 60–44, in the county tournament. The Earl Beagle squad was led by Carl Geis with 14 points.

January 17, 1987—Walker Beagle PFC, U.S. Marine Corps Silver Star recipient, dies.

January 18, 1859—Greensburg is incorporated as a city.

Thomas Hendricks. *Courtesy of Daniel Fayette.*

January 19, 1994—Larry Dwenger dies at the age of thirty. He was a five-time United Midget Racing Association champion and early car owner of NASCAR champion Tony Stewart.

January 20, 1891—Joseph Clarence Osborn of Clarksburg is born. He was part of Company F, Eighteenth Infantry, and died of meningitis on May 28, 1917.

January 21, 1950—The Burney Panthers defeat Jackson at the county basketball tournament, 42-40. Coach John Miesel's squad was led by Bud Williams.

January 22, 1958—Arthur Carter Stewart dies at the age of sixty-nine. He was an international award-winning farmer who established Stewart Seeds in 1918.

January 23, 1788—War of 1812 veteran Daniel McCormick is born. He died in Decatur County on April 11, 1849, and is buried at Union Baptist Cemetery.

January 24, 1937—This was known as "Black Sunday" during the 1937 flood. The streets of Greensburg were covered with more than four inches of slush. Three hundred refugees from river towns arrived the following day.

January 25, 1905—Thanks to a donation of $15,000 from the Andrew Carnegie Foundation, the Greensburg Public Library opens. Bessie

Carnegie Public Library. *Courtesy of Daniel Fayette.*

Monfort is the first director, and Will Cumback, former lieutenant governor, serves as the board president.

January 26, 1863—Oliver Andres, Eighty-Third Indiana, Company E, dies. He is buried at Mound City National Cemetery in Illinois.

January 27, 1944—Charles Shoopman, U.S. Army, 34th Infantry Division, 135th Infantry Regiment, is killed in action in Italy.

January 28, 1964—Interstate 74 in Indiana begins construction.

January 29, 1960—The Pirates score seven consecutive points in overtime to defeat Aurora, 71–66. It is their first win over Aurora since 1952. Leading the Pirates in scoring was Ray Catron with 25 points.

January 30, 1951—The Pirates got a big conference win over Franklin, 56–46, led by Jim Cuskaden and Harold Stier's 15 points. Their coach, Bill Berberian, left after three seasons and moved to West Lafayette. There, he developed the motion offense. The gym is named in his honor. The 1948 Purdue MVP was a member of both the Illinois and Indiana Basketball Halls of Fame.

January 31, 1963—Rear Admiral Oliver Owen Kessing dies. He served during World Wars I and II and was a member of the Legion of Merit.

February 1, 1860—An incredibly large flock of wild pigeons migrates through Greensburg, completely shutting out the sun for nearly an hour.

APPENDIX

February 2, 1951—The temperature in Greensburg falls to negative thirty-five degrees, the state record until 1994.

February 3, 1933—Elmer Bohman scores a county-high 28 points as the New Point Little Giants round ballers defeat Sandusky, 52–19.

February 4, 1837—With a population of eight hundred, Greensburg is incorporated as a town.

February 4, 1922—Decatur County Memorial Hospital opens.

February 5, 1793—Reverend John Rankin is born. Rankin was one of Ohio's leading abolitionists. His work as a conductor on the Underground Railroad was depicted in Harriet Beecher Stowe's book *Uncle Tom's Cabin*. He frequently visited the Sand Creek Presbyterian Church.

February 6, 1826—James Rankin is born. He served in the Thirty-Seventh Indiana, Company K, as a corporal. He was killed at the Battle of Peach Tree Creek on July 20, 1864, and is buried at Springhill Cemetery.

February 7, 1970—Greensburg High School graduate Bob Barker, while playing for the Indiana State Sycamores, had a career-high 35 points against Butler University.

February 8, 1923—Lieutenant Robert Miers is born. A member of Company B, Thirty-Eighth Infantry, he was killed in battle near Brest, France, on September 9, 1944.

February 9, 1928—The first Co-op in Decatur County is formed.

February 10, 1926—More than six inches of snow falls in Greensburg in thirty hours. Drifting snow disrupts bus and train service.

February 11, 1945—Fred W. Haley, U.S. Army Technician, Fifth Class, is declared missing in action and presumed dead in the South Pacific near New Guinea.

February 12, 1861—Abraham Lincoln stops in Greensburg on the way to his inauguration in Washington, D.C.

February 13, 1861—The Electoral College officially elects Abraham Lincoln as president of the United States. Casting Indiana's first Republican electoral vote was Abe's friend and Greensburg's own Will Cumback.

February 14, 1924—The silent movie *The Hoosier Schoolmaster* (set locally) premieres.

February 15, 1945—PFC Paul W. Brancamp is killed in an LAC landing on a beach on the island of Luzon in the Pacific.

February 16, 1937—The Pirate basketball team defeats a tough Connersville team, 21–12, behind Jimmy Mendenhall's 7 points. The Pirates went on to win the regional final, defeating Columbus, 32–25, behind Rollin McKim's 11 points.

Site of Abraham Lincoln's visit to Greensburg. *Courtesy of Daniel Fayette.*

February 17, 1967—Bob Barker's 45 points leads the Pirate basketball team over Seymour, 76–49. The Pirates would go on to win their second regional title in a row.

February 18, 1949—The Greensburg Pirates win the coveted South Central Conference basketball championship by defeating the Rushville Lions, 52–34. They were led by leading scorer Rex Pratt, who had 17 first-half points.

February 19, 2016—The independent movie *Dearest Jane*, filmed in Greensburg, makes its premiere at Greensburg High School.

February 20, 1870—Greensburg's gothic-style First Christian Church is dedicated.

February 21, 1890—The Greensburg City Council approves the first electric lights.

February 22, 1903—John Craven McQuiston, brigadier general of the 123rd Indiana Regiment, dies. He served as a staff officer during the surrender ceremonies between General Sherman and Confederate General Johnston in Raleigh.

February 23, 1946—The Sandcreek Indians basketball team defeats Greensburg, 43–40, under Coach Ray Horn to win the sectional. The team was led by Sheldon Stunkel with 15 points.

February 23, 2018—Greensburg Community High School graduate Sean Sellers set the Ball State University all-time record for the most three-point goals in one game, against Western Michigan.

February 24, 1951—After losing four previous sectional final games, Jackson defeats Greensburg, 59–58, thanks to a last-second shot by Don Hill.

February 25, 1924—Bill Berberian is born in Detroit. He received a Bronze Star in World War II, was a Purdue basketball MVP and coach at Greensburg High School from 1949 to 1953 and won a sectional and SEC title, then coached at West Lafayette for over thirty years. He had over four hundred wins and is a member of the Indiana Basketball Hall of Fame.

February 26, 1966—The Greensburg Pirates win their basketball sectional by defeating Milroy, 87–62, led by George Lanning's 20 points. This team would win their first regional since 1937 and lose in the regional final to Tech, 79–75. They were led by Terry Martin and Steve McCammon, with 21 points each.

February 27, 1896—Edward William Forkert is born. He served in the 1st Company, 1st Training Battalion, 159th Depot Brigade, as a technician fifth class. He died of disease on May 28, 1918.

February 28, 1970—In hoops action, the North Decatur Chargers, under Coach Dave Horn, win their first sectional by defeating Rushville, 73–70. They were led by Mark Wenning's 20 points.

March 1, 1941—The St. Paul Blasters under Coach Malcolm Clay defeat Greensburg, 33–24, for the basketball sectional title. They were led by Richard Garrett with 15 points.

March 2, 1896—Kid McCoy knocks out Tommy Ryan in the fifteenth round to win the world welterweight title. Primarily living in Rush County, he did live in Greensburg and took his nickname from McCoy Station.

March 3, 2021—Dr. Jane Goodall is the featured guest as Chautauqua moves to a live virtual experience due to the COVID pandemic.

March 4, 1945—Private First Class Willard Waters of Millhousen, Company L, Thirty-Eighth Infantry, Second Division, Patton's Third Army, is wounded in battle in Belgium. He died the next day.

March 5, 1982—The Greensburg Pirates' Bob Hubbard sinks two free throws to give them a 58–57 sectional championship win over North Decatur.

March 5, 1983—The South Decatur Cougar basketball team under Coach Dave Porter defeats Rushville, 43–42, led by Brian Proffitt, to claim the school's first sectional title.

March 6, 1987—The Elks building in downtown Greensburg collapses, killing one and injuring several.

March 6, 1988—Jon Taylor sinks a sixty-footer to give Coach Gary Cook's North Decatur Charger basketball team their second sectional championship, defeating Greensburg, 60–58.

March 7, 2019—Wentworth Press rereleased the 1906 book by George Cary Eggleston, brother of J. Edward Eggleston, *Jack Shelby*. The book is set in rural Decatur County. Longtime *Greensburg Daily News* writer Smiley Fowler was a consultant.

March 8, 1964—The Clarksburg Raiders lose in regional basketball action to Franklin by a mere 2 points, 69–67.

March 9, 1970—William Frederick Rondeau dies in service of his country in Germany.

March 10, 1984—Greensburg basketball coach Phil Snodgress coaches the Pirates to the regional championship with a 43–42 win on a last-second basket by John Ripperger.

March 11, 1984—Mary Lou Davis is named Mrs. Indiana.

March 12, 1921—The Sandusky Blackhawks defeat Evansville Central in the Bloomington basketball regional, led by P. Marlowe with 10 points. They were the first county school to win a regional title.

March 13, 1964—Dave Green, longtime Greensburg High School teacher and basketball coach, is a member of the Evansville Purple Aces NCAA Division II basketball championship team and helps defeat Akron, 72–59.

March 14, 1861—Dr. Richard Robbins dies in Greensburg. The doctor and lawyer was a member of the Indiana state senate and was a delegate to the first Republican Convention, held in Philadelphia. His picture hangs at the Indiana State Museum.

March 15, 1968—First Lieutenant Patrick Alan Shutters, twenty-one, the first Greensburg man to die in Vietnam, is killed at Thu Duc, Vietnam. He received both the Bronze and Silver Stars. He served in the U.S. Army, Company B, First Battalion, Eighteenth Infantry Regiment.

March 16, 2017—Bryant McIntosh, Greensburg High School graduate and member of the Indiana Basketball All-State team, leads Northwestern University, scoring 25 points as the Wildcats defeat Vanderbilt, 68–66, in the first round of the NCAA Tournament.

March 17, 1925—Private First Class Gerel Gibson, Second Marines Division, is born. The 1943 Burney graduate died on Saipan, Northern Marina Islands, on June 20, 1944.

March 18, 1945—Private First Class Howard R. Ruble, U.S. Army, 259th Infantry Regiment, 65th Infantry Division, is killed in action in Belgium.

March 19, 1947—Greensburg Community High School graduate Oliver Kessing is named deputy commissioner of the All-American Football Conference. Two years later, he was named commissioner.

March 20, 1917—Verne Starling Wamsley enlists in the U.S. Army Medical Corps. He died on January 18, 1919, of influenza.

March 21, 1931—The Greensburg Pirates, coming off a regional title, advance to the state finals at Butler Fieldhouse but lose, 31–18, to Terre Haute Wiley. Coach Frank Pruitt's team was led by Bob Oliger.

March 22, 1920—Madge Rutherford Minton is born in Greensburg. She was one of the first women in the United States to graduate from the Advanced Civilian Pilot Training Program and became a WASP in World War II.

March 23, 1836—The City of Westport is founded by Simeon Sharp.

March 23, 1944—Anne Frank's diary entry includes her eyewitness account of a U.S. plane crashing into a school near her hiding place. "The Germans shot at the airmen terribly," and two were killed. Decatur Countian Paul Geis survived this crash and was held as a POW.

March 23, 2013—Greensburg High School wins its first state basketball championship.

March 24, 1869—Future Lieutenant Governor Will Cumback is born in Franklin County, Indiana.

March 25, 1945—Private First Class William Holtzlider dies on Iwo Jima. He was nineteen years old.

March 26, 1800—Reverend Samuel Lowry is born. He trained under leading abolitionist Reverend John Rankin. Lowry was the first minister of the Sand Creek Church.

March 26, 1915—Carl Fisher's Miami Beach is opened for business.

March 27, 1920—Roderick Tetrick is born. He was a captain in the U.S. Army Air Corps and a recipient of the Air Medal.

March 28, 1796—John Thomson is born in Nicholas County, Kentucky. He and Elijah Mitchell put up the first wool carding machine four miles northeast of Greensburg between 1825 and 1826.

March 29, 2014—Greensburg wins back-to-back state basketball championships with an 89–76 win over Bowman Academy. Sean Sellers led the way with 27 points, and Collin Rigney chipped in 23 points.

March 30, 1946—Murle F. Wiley of St. Paul is listed as dead. He was a navigator on a B-24M, Tenth Air Force, Seventh Bombardment Group,

Ninth Bombardment Squadron. After his plane successfully bombed Rangoon Burma, the plane lost altitude and crashed on March 29, 1945. The crew was reportedly captured by the Japanese and was never heard from again. He received the Distinguished Flying Cross.

March 31, 1835—Thomas Hendricks, the founder of Greensburg and a colonel in the War of 1812, dies.

April 1, 1945—Private Curtis R. "Curt" Collins is killed in Germany.

April 2, 1862—Corporal Perry Brisbain, Fifty-Second Indiana, Company B, dies in St. Louis.

April 3, 1974—An F4 tornado goes through the southern part of Decatur County, killing two, including Emma Fry, and destroying 90 percent of Hamburg.

April 4, 1945—Sergeant Franklin K. Avery of St. Paul, fighting with the 378th Infantry Regiment, 95th Infantry Division, U.S. Army, is killed near Beckum, Germany.

April 5, 1918—Fred Leslie Luther of Burney dies of pneumonia while serving in the U.S. Navy. Luther served as a second-class officer, radio squad wireless operator.

April 6, 1862—As members of the Eighty-First Ohio, Elizabeth and John Finnern are at the Battle of Shiloh, the bloodiest two days in American history. Elizabeth dresses as a man in order to be with her husband. When her secret was detected, she stayed on as a nurse. They moved to Greensburg after the war and are both buried on the Soldiers Circle at South Park Cemetery.

April 7, 2021—The Spring Chautauqua features a live virtual concert from Germany with one of the world's premier opera singers, Megan Marie Hart.

April 8, 1892—Rose McConnell is born in Greensburg. She married Huey Long and eventually completed his term as U.S. senator after his assassination, becoming the third female U.S. senator.

April 9, 1976—On opening day for the Baltimore Orioles, New Point's Dyar Miller saved Jim Palmer's 1–0 victory by retiring future Hall of Famers Jim Rice, Carl Yastrzemski and Carlton Fisk.

April 10, 1949—After receiving the National Junior Chamber of Commerce's "City of Democracy" distinction, a $12,000 replica of the city is created thanks in part to a donation from the Ford Foundation. On this date, its first showing is held at the National Guard Armory, with some 3,500 people viewing it.

April 11, 1949—The "City of Democracy" model replica of Greensburg is flown out of the country for a European tour.

April 12, 1958—The ninth continuously growing tree on the courthouse tower, "old number 9," has to be removed for architectural reasons. Number 10 remained intact.

April 13, 1979—Walter Thomas Moore, World War I veteran of the U.S. Army, Thirtieth Division, dies. He was recognized by the French government for capturing thirty-five Germans single-handedly.

April 14, 1983—Ken Kercheval Day is celebrated at Greensburg High School. The star of TV's *Dallas* pays a visit.

April 15, 1726—The Pleak family of Decatur County traces their roots to Johann Pleak, who was born on this day in Holland.

April 16, 1907—The Lone Tree Chapter of the Daughters of the American Revolution is formed.

April 17, 1856—Henry Speed dies at the age of twenty-two. Speed has the only legible gravestone left in the African Methodist Episcopal Cemetery in Fugit Township.

April 18, 1847—Lieutenant William Sanders (Saunders) of the Mounted Infantry of Kentucky is killed during the Battle of Cerro Gordo, Mexico, during the Mexican-American War.

April 19, 1775—Samuel Lovejoy, a minuteman, fights General Thomas Gage's troops at Lexington, Massachusetts. He later settled in Decatur County. He died on August 24, 1837, and is buried at Star Baptist Cemetery.

April 19, 1859—With a population of around 1,200, Greensburg is incorporated as a city.

April 19, 1943—Mothers of World War II no. 66 meets at the Armory. The group had received national attention, giving special recognition to Mrs. Alvie G. Pratt, who had six sons serving in the armed forces.

April 20, 1863—John Shumm of the Sixty-Eighth Infantry is killed at the Battle of Nashville.

April 21, 1945—Lawrence Wolter, sergeant in the U.S. Army, is killed in action in Luzon, Philippines.

April 22, 1762—Joseph Lee is born in New Jersey. A Revolutionary War veteran, he later moved to Decatur County and died on August 24, 1837. He is buried at Shiloh Cemetery.

April 23, 1874—The Mount Arie Church is organized.

April 24, 1946—Bronze Star recipient and longtime community activist Morgan Miers marries Nansi Harris.

April 25, 1849—The Clarksburg Church of Christ is established.

April 26, 1943—Allied plans are laid out for the assault on Hill 609 in Tunisia against Germany's General Erwin Rommel. Among the soldiers was

Greensburg's Elmer Popejoy, a sergeant in the Thirty-Fourth Infantry Division and a recipient of both a Purple Heart and a Bronze Star Medal.

April 27, 1920—Roderick Tetrick is born. He was a captain during World War II, a member of the U.S. Army Air Corps and a recipient of the Air Medal.

April 28, 1896—Cy Bowen of Kingston makes his Major League Baseball debut with the New York Giants and strikes out three.

April 29, 1863—James, Hart, Seventh Indiana Infantry, gives his account of the Battle of Chancellorsville: "First shots fired from the enemy pickets at about 5 am. Succeeded in crossing about 12. Loss to us 10 or 12. The 4th Brigade crossed and took near 100 prisoners. The rebel pickets we killed and wounded near 30. Laid in line battle all pm."

April 30, 1917—Charles Thomas Link is born. During World War II, he served as a U.S. Army staff sergeant. He received two Battle Stars and a Bronze Star for personally bringing down four enemy planes in forty-three months in the Pacific theater.

May 1, 1879—Mary Stewart marries John Newman Carey. She was born in Greensburg, and the family moved to Indianapolis when she was three. She donated her home at 1150 North Meridian Street to the Children's Museum and founded the Indianapolis Children's Museum.

May 2, 1922—A resolution is called for to create the Greensburg Chamber of Commerce.

May 3, 1968—Senator Robert Kennedy campaigns in Greensburg.

May 4, 1919—James Ward, of Letts, one of two Decatur County POWs, is returned home after being held for six months.

May 5, 1861—Colonel Ira G. Grover is shot in the head and taken prisoner at the Battle of the Wilderness. He survived but died an early death because of his wounds.

May 6, 1918—Joseph W. Welsh is the first Decatur County soldier to be killed in battle during World War I.

May 7, 2014—After participating in the Greensburg Chautauqua, seven-time Emmy winner Ed Asner flies back to California.

May 8, 1911—Carl Fisher's Indianapolis 500 runs for the first time. Among the drivers is Fred "Skinny" Clemons, who is also from Greensburg and participates as a relief driver.

May 9, 1859—The first mayor of Greensburg, Richard Blair Thompson, begins his term in office.

May 9—Pat Smith's birthday. The prolific writer has had a column with the *Greensburg Daily News* for the past forty-six years.

May 10, 1891—Following the 1890 census, an area in Letts is determined to be the geographic center of the population of the United States. The commemoration event is held on this date.

May 11, 2010—Coach Bill Yoast, depicted in the film *Remember the Titans,* and Vince Papale, depicted in the film *Invincible,* inspires the student body at the North Decatur Chautauqua. Miss America, Katie Stamm, also speaks to the students.

May 12, 1864—Oliver Allan Owens, Seventh Indiana, Company D, dies from wounds suffered at Spottslyvania Court House.

May 13, 1949—Dale Gauck is born in Decatur County. As a U.S. Army sergeant during the Vietnam War, his commendations included two Bronze Stars and a Purple Heart.

May 14, 1822—The first county commissioners meeting is held at the home of Thomas Hendricks. Washington Township is formed.

May 14, 1900—John W. Shaw is killed in action in the Philippine Islands during the Spanish-American War.

May 15, 1927—The Greensburg Methodist Church is dedicated.

May 15, 1935—The movie *The Hoosier Schoolmaster* (set locally) premieres.

May 16, 1836—Revolutionary War veteran James Crawford dies. He was the first man buried in the Milford Cemetery.

May 17, 1920—John Layton, Greensburg resident, dies at the age of eighty.

May 18, 1971—The Tree County Players is formed, thanks to Cleo Duncan and Sue Burdett.

May 19, 1871—The first Greensburg High School commencement is held, with two graduates, Ida R. Stout and Anna Myers.

May 20, 1826—The Greensburg Presbyterian Church is founded.

May 20, 1830—Hugh Montgomery Sr., an early pioneer in Decatur County, dies. Born in Ireland, he fought for the Patriots in the Revolutionary War while his brothers fought for the British. He reenlisted for the War of 1812.

May 21, 1863—Reuben Smalley, with the Eighty-Third Volunteer Indiana Regiment, volunteers for a dangerous mission at Vicksburg. He was ultimately awarded the Medal of Honor for his actions.

May 22, 1863—Jacob Overturf receives the Medal of Honor due to his heroism at Vicksburg on this day.

May 23, 1931—Dr. Aldred Scott Warthin, GCHS class of 1884, known as the "Father of Cancer Genetics," dies.

May 24, 1856—Ira Hollensbe is born. The Greensburg entrepreneur built one of the first automobiles in the country, the Simplicity Horseless Carriage, in 1904, which he drove to the first Indianapolis 500 seven years later. He was a friend of Henry Ford, built radiators for him, and was the first Ford agent in Indiana.

May 25, 1917—Dana Harrold, corporal in the U.S. Army, Sixth Coast Artillery, dies of disease.

May 26, 1861—John Lugenbell is born in Greensburg. He served as captain of the fire department and was known for his skills in carriage painting.

May 27, 1918—Joseph Henry Kinker of New Point enters the service, Battery B, 142nd Field Artillery, 39th Division. He died of disease on September 19, 1918, in France.

May 28, 1945—Private First Class James Johnson sends his last letter to his mother. He was killed in fighting on Okinawa three days later.

May 29, 1921—James Johnson is born. A U.S. Army private, he was killed in action on Okinawa on May 31, 1945.

May 30, 1927—One-time Greensburg resident Wilbur Shaw races to a fourth-place finish in the Indianapolis 500 aboard Greensburg's Fred "Skinny" Clemons car, no. 29. It was Shaw's first 500.

May 31, 1937—Wilbur Shaw wins his first of three Indianapolis 500s. His formative teen years were split between Greensburg and Shelbyville.

June 1, 1861—The advance on Phillippi, aided by the Seventh Indiana, with Adjutant James Gavin, Captain James Morgan, First Lieutenant Ira Glanton Grover and Second Lieutenant Benjamin Ricketts, all of Decatur County, helps secure the separation of West Virginia from Virginia.

June 2, 1970—Corporal Kenneth Bernard Luttel is killed in action in Quang Tri, Vietnam. He was a member of the 501st Signal Battalion.

June 3, 1942—The turning point in the war against Japan during World War II, the Battle of Midway, begins. Among the pilots participating is Greensburg Community High School graduate First Lieutenant Jack Shriver.

June 4, 1861—Greensburg's John Wilder is promoted to lieutenant colonel.

June 5, 1918—Benjamin Turner Strain, U.S. Army, is killed at Chateau-Thiery. His heroism that day earned him the Distinguished Service Cross.

June 6, 1944—Kathryn Ernstes Bailey, a head nurse for the U.S. Army Nurse Corps, is in charge of one thousand beds during the D-Day invasion on the beaches of Normandy.

June 7, 1945—Ward Walter Farlow is listed as dead. He was a seaman first class, U.S. Navy, and went missing on D-Day, June 6, 1944.

June 7, 1966—Major John Charles Jacobs of Millhousen, a U.S. Air Force pilot, is killed in action at Phuoc Tuy Province, South Vietnam.

June 8, 1863—John Opel, Medal of Honor recipient, Seventh Indiana Regiment, captures the flag of the Fiftieth Virginia at the Battle of The Wilderness.

June 9, 1975—New Point graduate Dyar Miller makes his Major League Baseball debut with the Baltimore Orioles.

June 10, 1829—James Gilman Robbins is born in Decatur County. He and his sons, of J.G. Robbins and Sons, breeders of shorthorn cattle, won the herd prize at the 1893 Chicago World's Fair.

June 11, 1765—Thomas Donnell is born in Carlisle, Pennsylvania. He was an early settler of Kingston. He served from ages thirteen to eighteen as a frontier ranger and as a member of the Pennsylvania Militia.

June 11, 1840—George Rhiver is born. He was the owner of the newspaper *Decatur Republican* and was killed in action on April 21, 1862, as a member of the Greensburg Regimental Band.

June 12, 1915—Harry Wright is born. The World War II private first class, U.S. Army, was a Silver Star recipient.

June 13, 1860—Abraham Lincoln writes to his friend, Will Cumback, in part to gauge his chances of winning in Indiana.

June 13, 1959—The Greensburg centennial celebration begins.

June 14, 1822—With a population of 150, Greensburg is chosen as the county seat.

June 15, 1848—Major James Talbott, Indiana Infantry, U.S. Army, Sixteenth Regiment, is killed in Mexico during the Mexican-American War.

June 15, 1931—President Herbert Hoover pays a visit to Greensburg.

June 16, 1876—When it was clear that former Indiana Governor Oliver P. Morton would not be selected as the Republican Party's nominee for president, Will Cumback persuades the Indiana delegation to support Rutherford B. Hayes, ensuring his nomination for president.

June 17, 2013—Angela Gauck, North Decatur High School, wins the IHSAA golf championship.

June 18, 1924—Raymond Taylor is born. He was a member of the U.S. Army, 484th Ordinance Evacuation Company. He died on September 9, 1944.

June 19, 1846—The first officially recognized baseball game is played in New Jersey. Decatur County has had five major league baseball players: Janet Rumsey of Burney, Alex Meyer of Greensburg, Dyar Miller of New Point, Cy Bowen of Kingston and Bob Wright of Westport.

June 20, 1959—The Greensburg Centennial Parade takes place with movie star Miss Frances Farmer as the judge of the beard contest.

June 21, 1899—George Dilts is killed in the Battle of the Philippines during the Spanish-American War.

June 22, 1919—Lieutenant Robert Theodore Hall is born. He was listed as missing at sea on July 30, 1944. His name is listed on the Honolulu Memorial.

June 23, 1919—Earl Capper, Company A, 113th Field Signal Battalion, 38th Division, is stationed in Le Havre, France. His office receives the message of the signing of the Versailles Treaty, and Capper sends the message to the world.

June 24, 1922—Ward Walter Farlow, seaman first class, U.S. Navy, United States Naval Reserve, is born. His ship, *PC-1261*, was sunk off the English Channel during D-Day on June 6, 1944. He was presumed dead on June 7, 1945.

June 25, 1982—Westport Covered Bridge is placed in the National Register of Historic Places.

June 26, 2015—Alex Meyer makes his MLB debut with the Minnesota Twins as they face the Milwaukee Brewers.

June 27, 1911—Roy Hess is adopted by Mrs. Phamil Armstrong of Letts. He was a member of the World War I Gold Star Honor Roll. He died of disease in camp on October 27, 1918.

June 28, 1918—Benjamin Turner Strain, U.S. Marine Corps, Forty-Fifth Company, Fifth Regiment, receives the Distinguished Service Cross posthumously. He was killed in action on June 6, 1918, at Chateau-Thierry.

June 29, 1850—Revolutionary War veteran and first pioneer to settle in Adams Township, John Gullion, dies. He survived multiple gunshots through the cheek and mouth.

June 30, 2009—Norman Conrad Schlemmer Jr. dies. He was a first lieutenant in the U.S. Army, 3rd Platoon, K Co. 3rd Battalion, 394th Infantry Regiment, 99th Infantry Regiment. He was wounded during the Battle of the Bulge and received a Purple Heart and a Bronze Star.

July 1, 1911—The first Greensburg Chautauqua opens at Brachen's Woods.

July 2, 1982—The animated movie *The Secret of NIMH* premieres. Fred Craig is director of special processes and production manager.

July 3, 1938—Carl Fisher's Lincoln Highway opens. It was the nation's first east–west highway.

July 4, 1919—Tri Kappa Sorority hosts its first Fourth of July parade.

July 5, 1993—It is announced that longtime Greensburg High School band director Jerry Williams, along with two Tennessee lyricists, will share

$1,000,000 for winning a national patriotic music contest with their entry, "America, My America."

July 6, 1809—Luther Donnell, noted abolitionist, is born.

July 7, 1937—*The Hoosier Schoolboy*, set locally and starring Mickey Rooney, premieres.

July 8, 1906—Colonel Harold Braden Meek is born in Greensburg. Recipient of the Legion of Merit, he served in the USMC for thirty years in World War II and Korea with the Ninth Signal Battalion, and was at Guadalcanal, New Guinea and other Pacific locations.

July 9, 1926—Following a ten-day heat wave, a vicious storm hits the western part of Decatur County, moving buildings from their foundations.

July 10, 1943—Edwin Shireman, Sixty-Sixth Armored Division, participates in the invasion of Sicily. He was killed in battle on July 11, 1943.

July 11, 1996—Greensburg's Craig Houk fights boxing world champion Hector Camacho in New York's Madison Square Garden.

July 12, 1863—Scouts of Morgan's Raiders enter Decatur County at New Point. B.B. Harris, one of the scouts, would eye land near Letts and come back after the war and establish Harris City. Morgan never entered Greensburg, choosing to go east and then north into Ohio.

July 13, 1863—The city of Greensburg looks like a military camp as it prepares for a possible attack by Morgan's Raiders.

July 14, 1950—Charles Robert Low of Westport is killed in Korea.

July 15, 1918—Frank Joseph Wilmer of Millhousen, Company I, 166th Regiment, 42nd Division, is captured during battle at Champagne, France.

July 15, 1957—Surgeon General Dr. Leroy Burney (a Burney High School graduate) announces a link between tobacco and cancer, the first person to do so.

July 16, 1894—Clarence Everett Riley is born. He was a member of Battery A, 139th Field Artillery. He died of disease on December 9, 1917.

July 17, 1841—The Greensburg Baptist Church is organized.

July 18, 1849—Thomas Martin, Revolutionary War veteran, dies. He is buried in Springhill Cemetery.

July 19, 2017—Greensburg's Alex Meyer pitches seven innings, giving up only one hit with seven strikeouts for the Nationals, beating the Angels, 7–0.

July 20, 1918—Otis Clarence Jackson of Harris City, U.S. Army, Company M, Eighteenth Infantry, then Company D, Second Machine Gun Battalion, First Division, is killed in action at Chateau-Thierry.

July 21, 1969—Neal Armstrong and Buzz Aldrin take off from the moon on the lunar module *Eagle* to rejoin Michael Collins on *Columbia*. Woody Carr of Greensburg worked at the Indianapolis Detroit Diesel Allison plant that made the fuel tanks for *Eagle*.

July 22, 1918—Herman Andrew Vogel, a member of Battery B, Second Battalion, Field Artillery Replacement Depot, enlists. He died of influenza on October 12, 1918.

July 23, 1862—Sylvester Yoder, Fifty-Second Regiment, Company B, dies.

July 24, 1862—First Lieutenant Robert Braden, Seventh Indiana, Company D, is killed by Morgan's Raiders near Henderson, Kentucky.

July 25, 1914—Decatur County YMCA is first incorporated.

July 26, 1862—Lieutenant Robert Braden and James Pierce, Seventy-Sixth Regiment, Company D, drown at Cannelton, Indiana.

July 27, 1953—An armistice is signed, ending the war in Korea. Eleven Decatur Countians died during their service to our country.

July 28, 1950—Hailstones pile up in drifts as men who were threshing scoop up truckloads of them.

July 29, 1864—Daniel Anderson, Seventh Indiana, Company E, dies of disease at Salisbury, North Carolina. He is buried at Andersonville.

July 30, 1965—President Lyndon Johnson signs Medicare into law at the Truman Library. Present was Greensburg Community High School graduate Oscar Ewing, considered the "Father of Medicare."

July 31, 1935—A huge hailstorm strikes Greensburg at about 4:00 p.m. in a twenty-minute bombardment.

August 1, 1893—Private Joseph Henry Kinker of New Point is born. While serving our country in France during World War I, he died of pneumonia on September 19, 1918, and is buried at Oise-Aisne American Cemetery and Memorial in France.

August 2, 1895—William Harrison Ray is born. The Kingston World War I vet with Company C, Sixty-Seventh Infantry, died of pneumonia on November 12, 1918.

August 3, 1854—Decatur County pioneer Thomas Peevy dies. He is buried at South Park Cemetery.

August 4, 1823—The first election in Decatur County is held to choose a state senator and a county commissioner.

August 5, 1906—John Huston is born. The director, who won two Oscars and was nominated for fifteen, lived in Greensburg for a year. His grandmother lived here for many years, and his mother was born here.

August 6, 1900—W. Edward Metzler, Company L, Fourteenth Infantry, was killed in action during the Boxer Rebellion at Yang Taun, China.

August 7, 1964—James Turner, who served in the U.S. Navy in both world wars and received the Bronze Star, dies.

August 8, 1863—George Higgs, Sixty-Eighth Infantry, Company I, dies of disease in Tennessee. He is buried at Chattanooga National Cemetery.

August 9, 2016—The Decatur County Barn Quilt Trail kicks off as the county celebrates Indiana's Bicentennial.

August 10, 1876—Missionary Baptist Church is founded.

August 11, 1926—The Greensburg Country Club's original nine-hole course opens.

August 12, 1844—Revolutionary War veteran John DeMoss dies. He was buried at the Milton Byers Farm Cemetery. A volunteer in Virginia, he was at the Battle of Camden and then was a wagoner for the Marquis de Lafayette.

August 12, 1847—Revolutionary War veteran Samuel Jay Alley Sr. of Milford dies. He fought with Virginia troops.

August 13, 1950—Federal Security Administrator Oscar Ewing addresses the National Conference on Aging.

August 14, 1864—Evan Armstrong dies of disease at Waynesburg.

August 15, 1836—Young Decatur County pioneer Martha Kincaid dies at the age of twenty.

August 16, 1838—Judge W.A. Moore is born. He was twice elected to the Indiana House of Representatives and was once chosen for the Indiana Senate.

August 17, 1852—A passage from *Crossing the Plains*, a personal diary of his journey on the Oregon Trail, by Decatur Countian Origen Thomson: "We saw the grave of Mary Jane Watkins who had married Calvin Walker, one of their drivers. Since coming into the valley I have heard that in crossing the mountains he had lost both of the teams and had left the wagons and had since died."

August 18, 2021—The thirty-second annual Power of the Past Reunion kicks off.

August 19, 1896—W. Stewart Woodfill is born in Decatur County. He was the sole owner of the Grand Hotel on Mackinac Island from 1933 to 1979.

August 20, 1919—Observance of "Homecoming Day," as our troops who served in the Great War were welcomed home by fifteen thousand people.

August 20, 2011—Charles Buell Nature Trail is dedicated.

August 21, 1900—Edward Harbison boards the *Sherman* en route to the Boxer Rebellion. He served from 1890 to 1916. At that time, Harbison was the longest-serving Decatur Countian in continual army service.

August 22, 2021—The thirty-second annual Greensburg Power of the Past comes to a close after five days.

August 23, 1944—Oliver Kessing is promoted to the rank of commodore.

August 23, 1958—Tree no. 11 is discovered on the courthouse tower.

August 24, 1954—Burney's Janet Rumsey throws a no-hitter for the South Bend Blue Sox as they defeat the Grand Rapids Chicks.

August 25, 1835—The town of Milford is laid out by James Edwards.

August 26, 1775—John Kinkaid Sr. is born in Tennessee. The Decatur County pioneer died on August 9, 1848, and was buried at Springhill Cemetery.

August 27, 1966—Antique Car Day is celebrated as part of Indiana's sesquicentennial.

August 28, 1846—Revolutionary War veteran Benjamin Gosnell dies. He is buried in the Gosnell Cemetery.

August 29, 1993—The new Greensburg–Decatur County Public Library is dedicated.

August 30, 1862—Colonel James Gavin, commander of the Seventh Indiana Regiment, was shot in the chest at the Second Battle of Bull Run. He survived but was forced to resign.

August 31, 1996—Sandy Allen, *Guiness Book of World Records* holder for being the tallest woman, pays a visit to the Tree City.

September 1, 1969—Captain Robert P. Acher Jr. is killed in Long Khanh Province, Vietnam.

September 2, 1822—The first sale of lots occurred in Greensburg, all thirty-six on or near the public square. The most expensive was purchased by Thomas Hendricks for $121. That lot would become the DeArmond/Taylor Hotel.

September 3, 1853—Twenty-year-old H.C. Stockman arrives in town. He owned a sizeable grain business and served as Decatur County treasurer.

September 4, 1891—WAGR Homer Monroe Giddings, telegraph operator for Company M, 335th Infantry, then Supply Co. 120th Infantry, is born. He was gassed, recovered and then killed in battle on November 4, 1918, during the Battle of the Argonne Forest.

September 5, 1869—Greensburg High School opens its doors, with Rebecca Thomson as principal.

September 6, 1864—Peter Hamilton, of the Seventh Indiana Infantry, Company E, captured at Welson Railroad, dies of disease in Andersonville Prison.

September 7, 1918—Coach Dave Porter is born. The Westport High School grad had 447 coaching victories at Sandcreek, Jac-Cen-Del and South Decatur. He was inducted into the Indiana Basketball Hall of Fame. He led Jac-Cen-Del to the final eight in 1969.

September 8, 1921—The St. Louis Cardinals featuring Honus Wagner comes to town and wins an exhibition game against the semipro team the Greensburg Eagles.

September 9, 1944—Lieutenant Robert Miers of St. Paul, U.S. Army, Company B, Thirty-Eighth Infantry, is killed in action near Brest, France.

September 9, 1971—The Tree County Players' first production opens. The play was *Under the Yum Yum Tree*, and it was held at the Greensburg Junior High auditorium.

September 10, 1938—Miss Indiana, Helen Marie Emly of Letts, finished as a semifinalist in the Miss USA pageant.

September 11, 1822—A resolution is passed to create the first post office.

September 11, 1947—The Greensburg Pirates begin playing football again. The last team played in 1903. It was resurrected, thanks to Coach Tom Downey.

September 12, 1970—Sergeant Carl Joseph AmRhein, Company G, Ninth Infantry, Second Division, dies. He and Sergeant Frank Dullaghan received the Silver Star for fearlessly rushing machine-gun nests under heavy fire in front of their men.

September 13, 1919—Sergeant George Morgan is born. He died on January 10, 1944.

September 14, 1838—Revolutionary War veteran Thomas Meek dies. He is buried at Springhill Cemetery. He was a volunteer from Virginia in the war.

September 15, 1899—Private First Class William Baxter, Machine Gun Company, Sixteenth Infantry, First Division, is born. The St. Paul resident received the Silver Star for exceptional bravery on May 28, 1918, during the capture and defense of Cantigny under heavy enemy fire. He personally broke up five attacks before being killed in action.

September 16, 1758——John DeMoss is born. The Revolutionary War veteran settled in Decatur County and died on August 12, 1844. He is buried on the Milton Byers Farm Cemetery. Sadly, the stone is no longer there.

General John Wilder Monument. *Courtesy of Daniel Fayette.*

September 17, 1862—The Seventh Indiana is part of the Battle of Antietam, and the Union is victorious.

September 18, 1863—Just before the start of the Battle of Chickamauga, Wilder's Brigade plays a crucial role at Alexander's Bridge defending the crossing of West Chickamauga Creek and helps to prevent the Confederates from flanking the Union army.

September 19, 1939—The Tree Theater shows its first film.

September 20, 1852—The first Decatur County Fair is held.

September 21, 1896—Harold Addison Risk is born. He served in World War I with the 13th Company, 4th Battalion, 159th Depot Brigade. He died of pneumonia on October 13, 1918.

September 22, 1891—Reverend Joseph Tarkington dies and is buried at South Park Cemetery. His famous grandson Booth is on hand to help eulogize him.

September 22, 1958—President Harry Truman pays a visit.

September 23, 1943—The plane with First Lieutenant Jack Graham Shriver, pilot in the U.S. Army Air Corps, B-26C Marauder no. 41-35293, serving with the Fortieth Bomb Group, Forty-Fourth Bomb Squadron, crashes after takeoff in Pratt, Kansas.

September 24, 1949—Shriver Field is dedicated, named in memory of Paul and Jack Shriver.

September 25, 1947—Bluegrass Hall of Fame member Larry Sparks is born.

September 26, 1876—John Shaw is born. During the Spanish-American War, Shaw was killed in battle on May 14, 1900, at Augean, Mindanao, Philippines.

September 27, 1918—Glenn Randolph Trestor, second class seaman, U.S. Navy, dies of pneumonia.

September 28, 1937—U.S. Army Specialist Stanley Nevin Brown is born. The 1956 GCHS graduate died on March 7, 1962, in Seoul, Korea, as a result of a hemorrhagic fever.

September 29, 1877—Example of Decatur County's daily life from the diary of Willie I. Lowry: "I have been churning in the forenoon and this afternoon Jessie came here and I went home with her."

September 30, 1882—Joab Stout and others lay out the town of Letts.

October 1, 2015—Larry Sparks is inducted into the Bluegrass Hall of Fame.

October 2, 1918—William Theising of St. Maurice, 13th Company, 4th Training Battalion, 159th Depot Brigade, dies of influenza.

October 3, 1874—Arthur Hutchison is elected first fire chief just two months after the purchase of a steam fire engine.

October 3, 1941—*The Maltese Falcon*, directed by John Huston, premieres.

October 4, 1992—The Greensburg–Decatur County Public Library breaks ground on a new building on 2.6 acres purchased from the Odd Fellows Home.

October 5, 1918—Michael Herbert Landis, Company K, Twenty-Sixth Infantry, First Division, of Westport was killed in action in France.

October 6, 1864—Private Francis Barton, Fifty-Second Indiana, Company B, dies in St. Louis.

October 7, 1780—Revolutionary War veteran Lucius Tanner fights as a fifteen-year-old at the Battle of the King's Mountain under the direction of General Greene. He arrived in Decatur County in 1831 and is buried in Clay Township at the Mowrey Cemetery.

October 8, 1820—William James Robinson establishes a homestead in Adams Township. He will also set up a school for the area. One of the students was future vice president Thomas A. Hendricks.

October 9, 2008—Honda Manufacturing of Indiana begins production.

October 10, 1981—Ruthanne Gordon goes to work for WISH-TV Channel 8 in Indianapolis as a reporter, assignment editor and anchor.

October 11, 1863—Entry from James Hart's diary on this date. He served with the Seventh Indiana Volunteer Regiment. "I was detailed for picket. General Buford crossed the Rapidan yesterday. This morning he began the attack. The rebels crossed the river at Raccoon Ford. Came near cutting our cavalry off then a brisk fight ensued lasting till dusk."

October 12, 1944—Oakley Wells, U.S. Army Infantry, is killed in action in France.

October 13, 1971—Private First Class Ricky Alan Pate dies in a crash with four U.S. Army helicopter crew members near Chau Lang, Run, on a medivac mission.

October 14, 1918—Walter Roy Morgan, 29th Company, 8th Training Battalion, 158th Depot Brigade, dies of influenza.

October 15, 1918—Sergeant Lawrence Wolter, U.S. Army, is born. He was killed in action in Luzon, Philippines, on April 21, 1945.

October 16, 1944—Private First Class Ira Eiler is killed in action in Florence, Italy, during the Allied invasion of Italy.

October 17, 1918—Harry Tomson Carman of Burney, Student Army Training Corps, dies of influenza.

October 18, 1807—James Bradford Foley is born in Mason County, Kentucky. He moved to Greensburg in 1834. In 1857, he was elected to the Thirty-Fifth Congress.

October 19, 2003—Blessed Mother Teresa is beatified in St. Peter's Square. Leading the documentation of her miracles is Greensburg's Sister Sefapono (Maribeth Riedeman). Mother Teresa was canonized a saint on September 4, 2016.

October 20, 1862—Nicholas Butler of the Thirty-Seventh Indiana Infantry, Company E, dies of wounds and is buried at Washington City.

October 21, 1942—Private Charles Shoopman, U.S. Army, 34th Infantry Division, 135th Infantry Regiment, enlists. He was killed in action on January 27, 1944, and is buried in Italy.

October 22, 1944—Harold E. Boling, with the 442nd Bomber Squadron, 305th Bomber Group, is killed in action.

October 23, 1864—Colonel Marine Tackett of the Third Indiana helps lead the Union to an important western victory at the Battle of Westport in Missouri.

October 24, 1944—John Mitchell Purvis, U.S. Naval Reserve, gunner's mate third class, is killed in action at sea off the Island of Samar, Philippine Islands.

October 25, 1864—Native of Decatur County, James Dunlavy captures Confederate Major General John S. Marmaduke and receives the Medal of Honor.

October 26, 1985—Channel 4 late-night television horror host Sammy Terry pays a visit to the Tree City.

October 27, 1918—Roy Hess of Letts dies of disease while serving in World War I.

October 28, 1820—Thomas Hendricks purchases four eighty-acre tracts of land in Greensburg.

October 29, 1899—Cornelius Anderson, corporal in the Civil War, Company F, Twenty-Second Indiana Regiment, dies in Greensburg.

October 30, 1914—Sergeant Franklin Avery of St. Paul is born. He died on April 4, 1945, and is buried at the Netherlands American Cemetery and Memorial, Linburg, Netherlands.

October 31, 1847—An enslaved woman named Caroline and her four children escape from bondage in Kentucky. They make their way through the Kingston corridor of the Underground Railroad in Decatur County and eventually to freedom in Canada.

November 1, 1878—The first local telephone line is set up.

November 1, 1918—Gunnery Sergeant Fred Marlowe of the Sixth Regular U.S. Marines single-handedly captures eighty-four Germans and nine machine guns near St. George, France.

November 2, 1861—Sergeant Francis Wadkins dies of disease at Eldwater.

November 3, 1847—Luther Donnell rescues Caroline and her four children, all fleeing enslavement, who had been detained by Woodson Clark.

November 4, 1918—Homer Giddings of Westport dies in action in the Argonne Forest during World War I. He was a member of Company M, 335th Infantry, Supply Company 120th Infantry.

November 5, 1991—Shel Smith is elected for an unprecedented fourth term as mayor of Greensburg.

November 6, 1824—Decatur County holds its first presidential election. A total of 144 votes are cast and showed a preference for Henry Clay.

November 6, 1972—Mayor George Barnett declares this date "Stan Mavis Day" in honor of Mavis winning the Cross Country State Championship.

November 7, 1870—Reverend F.W. Pepersack begins preaching at the new St. Mary's Church of Millhousen.

November 8, 1841—Thomas Clendenning is born. He was killed in battle on March 6, 1864, in Nashville, Tennessee.

November 9, 1932—Greensburg records its first snowfall of the year.

November 10, 1918—John Martin Nesbit of Greensburg, Company A, 502nd Engineers, is killed in action in France.

November 11, 1918—The Armistice ends World War I. Decatur County had twenty-nine Gold Star Honor Roll members, those who died in service to their country.

November 12, 1918—Kingston soldier Clarence Everett Riley dies of pneumonia.

November 13, 1942—Lieutenant Commander Wendell Osborn of the USS *Juneau* goes down with the ship during the Battle of Guadalcanal. Osborn graduated from the U.S. Naval Academy in 1927, where he lettered in football. In all, 687 men were killed on the *Juneau*, including the five Sullivan brothers.

November 14, 2019—The Greensburg Chautauqua hosts legendary blues musician Mac Arnold and his band, Plate Full O' Blues, in concert.

November 15, 1918—Leslie Raymond Shazer of New Point dies of influenza. He was a member of the U.S. Marine Corps.

November 16, 1944—Private First Class Herbert Hahn, U.S. Army, is killed in action on Leyte, Philippines.

November 17, 1942—Corporal Lester Louis Picker of Millhousen, U.S. Army Air Corps, Gunner, 90th Bomber Group, Heavy, 400th Bomber Squadron, is killed in action.

November 18, 1902—Rear Admiral William "Skee" Lawrence Erdmann is born.

November 19, 1965—New Pirate basketball coach Keith Greve faces Rushville in his first game. Greve would lead them to back-to-back regionals in 1966 and 1967 and was later chosen as a member of both Butler University's and the Indiana Basketball Hall of Fame.

November 20, 1953—Jim Huber hits three baskets in a minute to send the game into overtime. The Pirates won the game, 77–72, behind Huber's 26 points. Carl Bode and Joe Westhafer were named to the SCC All-Conference Team, and Westhafer led the team with 358 points.

November 21, 1918—Three Decatur County men, Herbert Boling, Forrest Turner and Franklin Wilson, are witnesses to the surrender of the German fleet several days after the Armistice.

November 21, 1986—The movie *An American Tail* premieres. Fred Craig was director of special photographic effects and the supervising production manager.

November 22, 1968—In the first North/South Decatur basketball clash, the capacity crowd witnesses a narrow 48–47 Cougar victory. The Cougar's Steve Reed leads the scoring.

November 23, 1990—South Decatur defeats Southwood, 44–15, to win the Class A Football Indiana State Championship.

November 24, 1864—Alfred Austin, Fifth Indiana Cavalry, Company H, dies at Andersonville.

November 25, 1886—Vice president under Grover Cleveland, Thomas A. Hendricks, dies. One of his first jobs was as a teacher at the Greensburg Seminary. His uncle was the founder of Greensburg.

November 26, 2000—Paul Lavelle Hoban dies. He was a staff sergeant in the U.S. Army during World War II and a recipient of the Air Medal.

November 27, 1943—Fred Ivan Jessup dies in Carthage, Tunis, Tunisia, while serving his country during World War II.

November 28, 1917—Albert Maudlin, a sailor aboard the USS *Albert Watts*, survives after the ship is torpedoed by a U-boat. He was rescued off the coast of Gibraltar.

November 29, 1976—North Decatur wins its first girls' varsity basketball game, defeating New Palestine and led by Marcia Miller's 16 points.

November 30, 1950—Robert White is listed as missing in action while fighting the enemy in North Korea. He was a member of the First Battalion, Ninth Infantry Regiment, Second Infantry Division, and was presumed dead on December 31, 1953.

December 1, 1942—Private James Hampton, Clarksburg High School graduate, enters the U.S. Army. A member of Patton's Third Army, Tank Corps of the Armored Force, he was killed in action in France on March 19, 1945.

December 2, 1863—Louis J. Bruner, former Decatur County resident and recipient of the Medal of Honor, volunteers to pass through enemy lines at Walker's Ford, Tennessee, and conveys to a battalion information that enables it to reach safety.

December 3, 1923—Bob Williams is born. He wrote the sports column "Shootin' the Stars" for the *Indianapolis Star*. He is a member of the Indiana Basketball Hall of Fame and the author of the iconic book *Hoosier Hysteria*.

December 4, 1918—The Red Cross establishes a temporary hospital in the Elk's Building to combat the influenza outbreak.

December 5, 1939—On receiving a federal charter, the First Federal Savings and Loan Association is created.

December 6, 1861—John Howard, Seventh Indiana Regimental Band, is killed at Elkwater, Virginia.

December 7, 1933—At the age of fifteen, Gilman Stewart is named Junior Corn King of the United States.

December 7, 1941—Wallace Crawley and Robert Kramer both die on the USS *Arizona* during the attack on Pearl Harbor.

December 8, 1861—Private Robert Christian, Seventh Indiana, Company E, dies of disease in Philadelphia.

December 9, 1917—Pleasant Dennison of St. Paul enlists in the U.S. Navy as a carpenter's mate, first mate. He died of tubercular meningitis after serving in France.

December 10, 1917—John Martin Nesbit enters the service. A member of Company A, 502nd Engineers, he was killed in battle at Chateau-Thierry.

December 11, 1878—Beloved citizen Arthur Hutchinson dies. He was the owner of the woolen mill and, as fire chief, purchased the first fire engine.

December 12, 1892—Miles Meadows dies. He is buried in the Kingston Cemetery. Meadows was a free man of color who was a stalwart in the Underground Railroad.

December 13, 1949—Ben Gurion proclaims Jerusalem the capital of Israel. It's important to note the significant influence Oscar Ewing of Greensburg had on U.S. policy in the acceptance of the Jewish state.

December 14, 1963—Down 31–18 at halftime to Martinsville, Greensburg scores 27 points, and Alan McLaughlin scores at the end for the victory, 61–59.

December 15, 1871—The first edition of *The Hoosier Schoolmaster* is published. The bestseller was written by former Milford resident J. Edward Eggleston. It is set in the Milford area and is based on actual local events and experiences.

December 16, 1915—Thanks to the generosity of Nelson Mowrey, the Greensburg YMCA opens.

December 17, 1967—Private First Class James Nesbit, Ohio 1403 Om Company, recipient of the Legion of Merit for his service during World War II, dies.

December 18, 1966—While making a routine traffic stop, Indiana State Police Officer William R. Rayner, is shot and killed, leaving the community in shock and sadness. The assailant was shot and killed by Deputy David Blodgett.

December 19, 1864—Marion Anderson "led his regiment over five lines of the enemy's works, where he fell severely wounded." This occurred at the Battle of Nashville, and he received the Medal of Honor for his bravery.

December 20, 1906—Renowned local poet Grant Henderson is born. He wins first place in the Shamrock Poetry Club's state contest in 1948. His most noteworthy book is *Sunset in Enochsburg*.

December 21, 1972—It is announced that Greensburg Community High School graduate, Marine Captain John Fogg, has been chosen to fly with the Blue Angels. He had flown 117 combat missions.

December 22, 1943—Tech Sergeant Oscar "Junior" Robbins Jr. is shot down over The Netherlands.

December 23, 1822—Joseph Snelling buys fifty-six acres of land in Fugit Township. He is one of the earliest land owners and a free Black man.

December 24, 2011—The *Greensburg Daily News* Cheer Fund marks its one-hundredth anniversary of delivering gifts and food to families in need throughout Decatur County. The early vision of Mabel and James Caskey, Walter Lowe and later Lori Durbin was invaluable to the organization's continued mission.

December 25, 1815—Gilbert Van Camp is born. He worked as a tinsmith just outside of Greensburg from 1845 to 1860. The next year, he moved to Indianapolis and began his canning business.

December 26, 1942—Sergeant Paul Sanders Shriver, US Army Air Corps, is killed in action in the Pacific theater.

December 27, 1944—The encirclement of Bastogne is broken as the Fourth Armored Division moves up from the south. With American units pushing from the north and south, the German advance stops, and the Bulge is contained. Among the local soldiers at the Battle of the Bulge were Joe Kneuven and Bronze Star/Purple Heart recipient Marlin Maddux.

December 28, 1862—Horatio May, Sixty-Eighth Infantry, dies at Andersonville Prison.

December 29, 1893—Wilber Kendal, member of the Indiana Journalism Hall of Fame, is born in Greensburg. In 1923, Kendal and some investors established the Greensburg Daily News Printing Corporation.

December 30, 1875—W. Edward Metzler, Company L, Fourteenth Infantry, is born. He was killed on August 6, 1900, in battle at Yang Taun, China, during the Boxer Rebellion.

December 31, 1863—The following soldiers from Decatur County, all part of the Fifty-Second Regiment, Company B, froze to death at Island # 10–Fort Pillow: Captain Edwin Alexander, David Dean, William Falconbury, George Havelin, William Tyler and George Wilson.

BIBLIOGRAPHY

Deiwert, Winona Crisler. *Decatur County in the World War*. Greensburg: Published by Order of the County Board of Commissioners of Decatur County, Indiana, 1922.

Ford, William A. *Lest We Forget*. N.p.: no publisher, 1997.

Harding, Lewis. *A History of Decatur County*. Indianapolis, IN: B.F. Bowen and Company, 1915.

Metz, Rheadawn, and Diana Springmier. Decatur County History. Dallas, Taylor Publishing Company, 1984.

Poore, Jack. *Decatur County Basketball*. Greensburg, IN: self-published, 1998.

Shirk, Lorene E. *Schools in Decatur County, Indiana: 1820–1978*. Greensburg, IN: Rural Couples Club, 1979.

Smith, William O. *A Brief History of the Underground for Escaping Slaves in Decatur County*. Decatur County, IN: self-published, 2007.

Thomson, Origen. *Crossing the Plains*. Fairfield, WA: Ye Galleon Press, 1896.

John and Rex Pratt. *Author collection.*

ABOUT THE AUTHOR

*J*ohn Pratt is the U.S. history teacher at Greensburg High School. His teaching career began fifteen years ago at North Decatur High School. He is a graduate of Greensburg High School and received his BA in history from Thomas More College. He and his wife, Jill, have two amazing daughters, Clare and Caroline.

His love of local history goes back to his childhood, when he found out that his idol, Abraham Lincoln, had a good friend from Greensburg, Will Cumback. His love of history has helped him develop noteworthy experience-based learning activities for his students. He has hosted twenty-seven Chautauqua events and over four hundred student-driven interviews with historically or culturally significant people, overseen a student renovation of an AME cemetery and raised funds for a Medal of Honor marker at South Park Cemetery. His awards include the Caleb Mills Indiana Historical Society's Teacher of the Year Award and the Indiana DAR's Teacher of the Year Award. He was also a recipient of a Lilly Creative Teacher Fellowship.